THE VALOUR OF FAITH

The Valour of Faith
The Gospel in the Life of Gideon

George Albert Rogers

CountedFaithful

THE VALOUR OF FAITH
From an edition published in 1859
This edition © Counted Faithful, 2017

COUNTED FAITHFUL
2 Drakewood Road
London SW16 5DT

Website: http://www.countedfaithful.org

ISBN
Book: 978-1-78872-018-2
ePub: 978-1-78872-019-9
Kindle: 978-1-78872-020-5

Contents

"Faith may rise into miracles of might, as some few wise men have shown:
Faith may sink into credulities of weakness, as the mass of fools have witnessed.
Therefore, in the first, saints and martyrs have fulfilled their mission,
Conquering dangers, courting deaths, and triumphing in all."

1

Invisible Might

"The Lord is with thee, thou *mighty man of valour.*"
"The Lord *looked* upon him, and said, Go in *this thy might.*"
"Surely I will be *with* thee." (*Judges 6:12, 14, 16*)

> "... Thou my all
> My theme! My inspiration! And my crown!
> My strength in age! My rise in low estate!
> My soul's ambition, pleasure, wealth! My world!
> My light in darkness! and my life in death!
> My boast in time! bliss through eternity!
> Eternity too short to speak thy praise,
> Or fathom thy profound of love to man!"

THE Bible is full of history. Whole books of the Scriptures are dioramic pictures of real life. God graciously meets our felt need in the Word. Facts make deeper impressions than precepts. We can remember them better. We need them both. In the Scriptures both are given to us.

No records of story are so true to life, none so interesting, none so pictorial, as those of the Bible. Life is real in the Word of Life. Life breathes therein. So exactly do its great living facts illustrate great principles, that some men, destitute of spiritual faith, have questioned the reality of the facts, in their admiration of the reality of their principles. Infatuated presumption! Truth borrows no light from falsehood. Eternal principles are not built upon the baseless fabric of fiction.

Bible pictures are not ideal portraits. They are the true photographs of realities. Creation, the fall, redemption, and all minor outlines, are portrayed before our eyes, just as they occurred. They are living and breathing upon the tablets of the Word, in all their original truth-fulness. Their colouring is as fresh as ever. Time does not dim them. Eternity will not destroy them. Were every Bible swept into oblivion, the facts recorded therein would be facts still. Neither prejudice nor ignorance, false philosophy nor mystic sentimentalism, nor height nor depth, will ever obliterate a single line of inspiration. It is eternal truth, and truth for eternity.

We propose to take down one portrait from the picture gallery of the Word, and examine it with the eye of faith. Rich truth will unfold itself in the brief outline of Gideon's history. We shall endeavour to fix attention upon a few of the most prominent features in his life. The development of great principles will be our aim. The drapery of narrative will be our illustrations.

In the opening of his story, we plunge at once into some of the deepest depths of Christian experience. And yet this experience is pictured out so simply before the mind's eye, that a child may read it. Truth is ever simple in proportion to its importance. We mark at once the inner soul of the believer in Jesus, who, compared with earth's mightiest heroes, is ever a "mighty man of valour."

But what believer truly and fully knoweth *himself*? Who can apprehend what Christ is to the true child of God? Mark, then, in the opening of Gideon's history – 1. *Valour Unknown*. 2. *Valour's Weakness*. 3. *Valour's Might*.

Valour Unknown

Gideon was pronounced by the angel who appeared unto him as "a mighty man of valour." But did Gideon know his own might? It would seem that, as a valorous man, he was as much unknown to himself as he was unknown to Israel, or to his enemies. His valour was real, but untried. His valour was living, but dormant. His valour was mighty, but unexercised. His valour was known in heaven, but on earth it was hidden, secret, unknown. His valour, too, was needed, but no man thought of him; he thought not of himself, as Israel's deliverer. His valour, like the pearl buried under the bars of the stormy deep, was lying, buried under the surging billows of oppression which now afflicted his fatherland.

Oft, too, is valorous faith unknown until it is tried. Great occasions make great men. Great trials make great believers. Faith as a grain of mustard-seed, is as strong in its principle, as is the faith which moves a mountain. But it needs growth, and development. The worm Jacob threshes the mountains, not by his own strength, but by the might of Him who holdeth his right hand. Unconscious strength is often the most potent. You cannot cast him down who is already low. You cannot rend him from the Rock of Ages, who is resting on Christ, as "the chief of sinners." There is unspeakable comfort in the fact that this "man of valour" was unconscious of his might, until the angel revealed to him his secret power. Many a faint-hearted believer is "overcoming the world" (*1 John 5:4, 5*) *unconsciously* to himself. His might is hidden, but it is no less real. Oppressed, he cannot be subdued. "Fightings without and fears within" – he reads bitter things against himself, but God calls him "more than conqueror."

No *created angel* was this, who revealed Gideon's might and valour unto him. The angel who spake was none other than the Lord, Jehovah, who "looked upon him," and said, "Have not I sent thee?" – (*verse 14*). He was the same speaker, too, who said, "Surely *I* will be with thee." (*verse 16*). It was this same angel-man over whom Jacob had power, and prevailed: "He wept, and made supplication unto him: he found him in Bethel, and there he spake with us; even the LORD God of hosts: the LORD is his memorial." (*Hosea 12:4, 5*)

Jesus thus appeared to the Old Testament saints as "the angel of the everlasting covenant." "Abraham rejoiced to see His day, and he saw it, and was glad." David sang of Him, when He celebrated His praises, and said, "The LORD said unto My Lord." Both in human and in angelic form, did He reveal Himself to the elder Church. Having in the fulness of time become incarnate, this marvel of condescension was eclipsed. He who stooped to *become* man, might well be supposed to have appeared *as* man. This great fact casts New Testament light upon the Old Testament pages.

It stereotypes the truth, that there has been from the first, but "one Lord, one faith, one baptism." Salvation, and the way of salvation, were revealed in Eden. Then the Sun of righteousness shed forth his morning light upon the Church. Soon will He appear in His meridian glory. But He has never set. Brightened by His light the Old Testament Scriptures sparkle with evangelical gems. But deny that He is as much the sum and substance of the Old Testament, as He is of the New, you blot the sun out of the heavens, you necessitate two centres to one perfect circle of truth.

9

It was this glorious angel who revealed Gideon to himself, as a "mighty man of valour." *He* knew what he was, for *He* made Him all he *could be.* Nor was it merely by His "appearing" unto him, that Gideon was aware of his might. The glorious appearing of the Lord Jesus to Saul, on his road to Damascus, prostrated him in the dust. It was his *word* which raised him up, and strengthened him. Thus Gideon knew not his might until the words of truth fell like electric power upon his ears, "The Lord is with thee, thou mighty man of valour."

"The entrance of thy words giveth light:" so spake the Psalmist, and so experiences every downcast believer. We know not that we have strength, much less do we know wherein our great strength lieth, until the entrance of the Word of God giveth light unto our souls. When that light cometh, then strength is revealed. May the Word assure the weakest saint who reads these pages, that God hath laid strength, upon One who is mighty.

But no sooner is Gideon told of his strength, than his weakness appears. This we shall soon discover when we notice,

Valour's Weakness

The sun is often behind a cloud. So is faith. The cloud, however, does not change the nature of the sun. Nor do beclouding dispensations, which chill the soul, affect the true nature of its faith. The Christian is often a paradox to himself. He is weak, and strong, at the same moment. "When I am weak, then am I strong," said one of the greatest believers. "It is the *nature* of faith, not the *quantity*, which determines the character," said an eminent divine; and, he added, "Samson was a riddle to me, till I unriddled myself. He was an inconsistent believer." Gideon is named with Samson among the mighty believers in *Hebrews 11.* We shall now see his inconsistent weakness. The causes of it are laid open before us.

He was now *walking by sight, and not by faith.* He could see no tokens of the Lord's presence: and, therefore, in reply to the salutation, "The Lord is with thee, thou mighty man of valour," he said, in the weakness of unbelief, "Oh! my Lord, if the Lord be with us, why, then, is all this befallen us? And where be all the miracles which our fathers told us of, saying, Did not the Lord bring us out of Egypt? But now the Lord hath forsaken us, and delivered us into the hands of the Midianites."

There was a strange amount of unbelief in all this. He seemed to call in question the Lord's truthfulness. "*If* the Lord be with us!" Thus unbelief always aims its shafts at the Lord's veracity. "Yea, hath God said?" whispered the serpent into Eve's ear. Once suffer doubt to hint at the bare possibility that it may not be exactly true in all cases, at all times, that "God is not a man, that He should lie," and faith will lose its foothold, and stumble.

Gideon overlooked God's justice, and man's sin. "Why, then, is all this befallen us?" The reason was patent. Surely Gideon could not have closed his eyes to all the idolatry in the land! Did he not know that his own father was a worshipper of Baal? Had sin become so familiar to him that its guilt, and desert, were obliterated from his mind? When faith's eye gets accustomed to the sight of sin, it grows dim. Once admit the slightest apology for the smallest sin, and the progress of unbelief is certain. Step by step the soul recedes from the light of Calvary. Darkness comes over it. And at length, when Justice unsheaths her sword in some sore judgment, the weak believer exclaims, "Why is all this befallen us?"

The chastisement of the Lord's people may often be traced up to the same cause. Does the afflicted child of God ask, "Why is all this befallen me?" He need not question the cause. It is not because the Lord is not with him. Far from it. It is the true vine that is purged. The barren fig-tree is plucked up by the roots, and cast away. But there is some evil permitted, some idol worshipped, some idolatrous altar erected. Search your heart, and you will not wait long for an answer to the question, "Why is all this befallen me?"

Hard thoughts of God were mixed with Gideon's faith. "Now the Lord hath forsaken us," he murmured. Was this true? The Lord had just sent a prophet to them, in answer to their prayer (*verses 7, 8*). Israel had forsaken the Lord, but the Lord had not forsaken Israel. His rod over them proved that He had not given them over to their sins. He had not yet said, "Ephraim is joined to idols, let him alone." David also murmured hard thoughts of the Lord, when, being hunted like a partridge upon the mountains, he exclaimed, "I shall one day perish by the hands of Saul." Let the enemy once persuade the doubting Christian that "the Lord hath forsaken him," and all his strength will vanish in a moment, and he will become an easy prey to all kinds of temptations. The Psalmist deeply felt this danger when he said, "Mine enemies speak against me; and they that lay wait for my soul take counsel together, saying, God hath forsaken him: persecute and take him; for there is none to deliver him." (*Psalm 71:10, 11*). But, on the contrary, how mighty is the weakest faith which clings to the presence of the Lord! Paul felt this. He urges Christians to realise the power of the promise, "I will never leave thee, nor forsake thee." Upon that promise he grounds his faith, and affirms, "So that we may boldly say, The Lord is my helper, and I will not fear what man shall do unto me." (*Hebrews 13:5, 6*).

False humility was another ingredient in the weak faith of Gideon. "Thou shalt save Israel," said the Lord: "have not I sent thee?" This two-fold promise should have been enough for any emergency. What could a creature need more? But Gideon, instead of fixing his eye of faith upon the Lord alone, began to think of himself. And he said, in reply, "Oh my Lord, wherewith shall I save Israel? Behold, my family is poor in Manasseh, and I am the least in my father's house." (*verse 15*). Wherein would his confidence have been placed had his family been the *richest* in Manasseh, and he the *greatest* in his father's house? There was a leaning to the arm of flesh in all this. This seeming humility and diffidence came not from above. Godly humility accounts God everything, man nothing. Even Moses, that meekest of men, failed here. "Come now," spake the Lord unto him, "I will send thee unto Pharaoh." "Who am I, that I should go unto Pharaoh?" replied Moses. And then, when the Lord told him what he should do, and say, he called in question both the Lord's wisdom and power, in making choice of him for the mission.

"Oh my Lord," he objected, "I am not eloquent, neither heretofore, nor since thou hast spoken unto thy servant: but I am slow of speech, and of a slow tongue. And the Lord said unto him, Who hath made man's mouth? or who maketh the dumb, or deaf, or seeing, or the blind? have not I the Lord?" Unbelief still objected. Human sufficiency still obtruded itself. Self must have a voice in the question. Moses would appear to know better than God, *who* should be chosen for this work. "Now therefore go," said the Lord, "and I will be with thy mouth, and teach thee what thou shalt say." And he said, "O my Lord, send, I pray thee, by the hand of him, whom thou wilt send. And *the anger of the Lord was kindled against Moses.*" (*Exodus 4:10-14*).

"Proud humility" is a fearful bane of the soul. It apes the most retiring and modest graces of the spirit; but it usurps the throne and sovereignty of Jehovah. Under its mask Satan robs believers of their comfort, and the Church of their zeal. Were the *creature* made *nothing*, and Jehovah *everything*, what Goliath could resist the sling and the stone of the veriest stripling? *Mock humility* cripples the energies of the Church of God. Many a victorious David would appear, many a Moses would grow eloquent, many a Gideon would rise up as a "mighty man of valour," were the egotism of pride laid low in the dust. The perpetual inquiry, "Who am *I*, that *I* should go?" paralyses faith in its first acts of obedience.

But now, we turn, and behold

Valour's Might

Gideon was "a mighty man of valour," notwithstanding all the weakness of his faith. We naturally ask wherein was his might? What was its source? In himself he was as weak as a babe.

The Lord's presence was one great source of valour's might. "The Lord is *with thee.*" "Surely I will be *with thee*," Here was might irresistible. No enemy can withstand the presence of the Lord. This presence is a panoply which no fiery darts can penetrate. Safety and victory are ensured as soon as the presence of the Lord is ensured. The weakest is strong in this strength. The babe has more than a giant's might. "Fear thou not; for I am with thee; be not dismayed; for I am thy God: I will strengthen thee: yea, I will help thee; yea, I will uphold thee with the right hand of my righteousness." (*Isaiah 41:10*).

The Lord's look was another source of valour's might. "The Lord *looked* upon Gideon, and said, Go in this thy might." The Lord's look of grace and love imparts strength to the soul. His look of anger strikes terror into the stoutest heart. "The Lord looked upon the host of the Egyptians through the pillar of fire and of the cloud, and troubled the host of the Egyptians." When the Lord setteth his face against a man, his strength dries up like a potsherd. That look withered Judas in a moment, and pierced him through with the anguish of utter despair.

But the "*look*" of love, revived the fallen Peter, and broke open the full fountain of his heart. Israel's victories are attributed to this same look. "They got not the land in possession by their own sword, neither did their own arm save them: but thy right hand, and thine

13

arm, and *the light of thy countenance.*" (*Psalm 44:3*). This "look," is sufficient to meet all emergencies. It chases away the darkest and thickest clouds. It is the sun rising in his strength, and shedding forth the penetrating and invigorating rays of his brightness. The weakest saint beaming, as did the face of Stephen, with the smile of Jesus, is mightier than the mightiest of earth's potentates. None can resist his power, nor gainsay his security and salvation. Death itself will only add wings to the chariot wheels of his faith. Be it so, that he is living in the midst of enemies. Be it so, that, like Paul of old, no man stands by him, and that all human aid fails him. This "look" of the Lord, fixes him for ever, as a star in the firmament of grace. His light will never be extinguished. He may rise above every storm, and boldly confront the world. "There be many that say, Who will show us any good? LORD, lift thou up the *light of thy countenance upon us.*" (*Psalm 4:6*).

The Lord's promise was one chief source of valour's might. Faith lives upon promise. It is its food and daily sustenance. It is the very sinew of its might. "Surely I will be with thee, and thou shalt smite the Midianites as one man." "Thou shalt save Israel." These were the promises with which Gideon was to wage war, and overcome. Promise is to faith, what the rope is to the drowning man. Faith begins to rise from despair to hope, by promise. Promise descending into the heart of faith, rises like water to its own level; and upbears the reposing soul to the very throne and bosom of God. Promise, like light issuing from the sun, cannot be polluted by earth's contamination. It is pure in whatever degree it shineth. It cometh from one source, and tendeth to one end.

The command of the Lord, no less than His promise, was the warrant of faith, and a chief source of valour's might.

"Go," saith the Lord. "Have not I *sent* thee?" The Captain of our salvation speaks as one having authority. Who can resist his will? Does He say, "Go"? Who then shall be able to prevent, or hinder, the servant in doing his Master's behest? Does he say, "Go," without providing "grace and strength," equal to the need of going? True faith is an obedient grace. Let but the Lord issue his command, and faith will answer, "Speak, Lord, for thy servant heareth." The Lord's command is faith's commission for undertaking the mightiest enterprises. At his word oceans have been crossed, deserts trod, ice and snow encountered, the wrath of man subdued, the powers of hell defied, and the victories of the cross won.

Here, then, is wisdom. Let the reader learn the source of *invisible might*. The question at issue, is for eternity. The interests involved, are the dearest of those upon which the mind of man can fix itself. No man can be in a negative state; no man living stands upon neutral ground. We are conquering, or being conquered. We are living or dead. We are rising or falling. "The Lord is *with* us," and we are mighty in the valour of faith; or the Lord is *against* us, and we are weakness itself, and an easy prey to the enemy, through the impotency of unbelief.

2

The Sign

"If now I have found grace in thy sight, then *show me a sign*
that *thou* talkest with me." (*Judges 6:17*)

"Thou art unchanged – thy gracious ear,
　　Still lists the cry of grief;
'Lord, I believe' – oh, deign to hear!
　　'Help thou mine unbelief.'
I know – I know thou wilt not spurn,
One who before thy cross would mourn.

"Increase my weak, my wavering faith,
　　Fix it on Thee alone;
Lead me to conquer sin and death,
　　And foes to me unknown;
Feeble and faint my cry may be,
Yet, Lord, I still would cling to Thee."

WHEN the Lord Jesus had risen from the dead, and first
appeared to his disciples, "they believed not for joy, and
wondered." Their doubts, however, were soon removed by the sign
which the Lord afforded them. He at once gave them the most
satisfactory evidence that it was really He, and no mere spirit, who
was talking with them. "Have ye here any meat?" said He unto them;
"and they gave him a piece of a broiled fish, and of an honeycomb.
And He took it, and did *eat* before them."

We may well imagine that the feelings of Gideon were not altogether dissimilar to those of the disciples of our Lord, when the angel
"looked upon him and said, Go in this thy might, and thou shalt save
Israel from the hand of the Midianites: have not I sent thee?" These

tidings were so welcome, and yet so marvellous, that Gideon's faith staggered. He "believed not for joy, and wondered." And then he sought "*a sign*," to satisfy himself that he was in a waking state, that his senses were not deceiving him, and that the angel was not a mere phantom called up by a heated imagination. "Show me *a sign* that thou talkest with me."

Now the sign which was given to Gideon was not altogether unlike in character, to the sign which our blessed Lord gave to his disciples, on his resurrection morn.

"Depart not hence, I pray thee," said Gideon to the angel, "until I come unto thee, and bring forth my present, and set it before thee. And he said, I will tarry until thou come again … And Gideon went in and made ready a kid, and unleavened cakes of an ephah of flour: the flesh he put in a basket, and he put the broth in a pot, and brought it out unto him under the oak, and presented it. And the Angel of God said unto him, Take the flesh and the unleavened cakes, and lay them upon this rock, and pour out the broth. And he did so. Then the Angel of the Lord put forth the end of the staff that was in his hand, and touched the flesh and the unleavened cakes; and *there rose up fire out of the rock*, and consumed the flesh and the unleavened cakes. Then the Angel of the Lord departed out of his sight. And when Gideon perceived that he was an angel of the Lord, Gideon said, Alas, O Lord God! for because I have seen an angel of the Lord face to face. And the Lord said unto him, *Peace be unto thee; fear not: thou shalt not die.*" (*verses 18-23*).

In both cases the emblems of peace and friendship were presented. In both cases the offering was accepted. In both cases it was *consumed*. The Angel consumed it, by "fire rising up out of the rock;" the Lord Jesus, by eating. In each instance, a satisfactory and conclusive *sign* was given, that it was none other than the Lord himself, who was speaking, and who had come down to deliver his people.

Now, do not *we* need some *sign* that the Lord talketh with *us*, and hath come down to "save *us*, from the hand of our enemies?"

Our enemies are many and powerful. Cruelly have they oppressed us. The Midianites of our hearts and the world, have often robbed us of peace and happiness, and continually bring us into bondage. They are oppressors, hard taskmasters. They would fain leave no sustenance for us. Baal cannot save us. Our idols cannot help us. In our despair we turn unto the Lord. We cry unto Him to come down and help us. He answereth our prayer. He sendeth a prophet to rebuke us for our iniquities, and to deepen our sense of sin. We are overwhelmed, we feel that we richly deserve all the affliction, and trouble which have befallen us. We turn our eyes to heaven, when lo! the bow of the covenant gradually forms itself upon our falling tears. When we expect death, the angel of mercy visiteth us! He talketh with us. He telleth us that the Lord is all mercy, all grace, all love to them that seek Him. He assureth us that the Lord will pardon all our sins, and take away all our iniquities; yea, He even affirmeth that the Lord will deliver us from all our enemies, and will make us more than conquerors, and at length put a crown of pure gold upon our heads! The glad tidings, we think, are too good to be true. We are incredulous. We cannot believe that all we hear is not a mere delusion. We fear to trust our own senses. We tremble lest we should be deceiving ourselves with false hopes. We want a sign that the Lord himself does indeed talk with us, and that He has indeed revealed Himself to our souls as the God of our salvation. And that sign He has surely given to us. Not a sign which can be seen by our eyes of sense, but a sign which shineth in characters of light before the open eye of faith. We need not now some audible voice, nor midnight dream, nor open vision to assure us of pardon and salvation. Jesus Himself has given us a sign. We see it on Calvary's hill. He has gone up upon the high rock of eternal justice, and upon that hard and bare rock, He made Himself more bare than it. He placed thereon his own flesh, and poured out thereon his own blood, and made thereon his own soul an offering for sin, and out of that rock arose fire – such fire as never had been kindled before, and that fire consumed the offering, and would have consumed Him who offered it, had He not been more than man. And as the cloud of that sacrifice arose from off the high altar-rock, Jesus did spread forth his hands and bless his people, and ascend in the cloud, and angels welcomed Him back to his throne and his "glory, which He had with the Father before the world was."

Let us draw near and see this great sight. Behold, the place whereon we stand is holy ground! Help us, O Spirit of Holiness, to put off our shoes, and stand with all humility at the foot of this rock.

We shall not fail to notice a three-fold character in this sign: 1. *It was an Appeal to the Senses.* 2. *It was a Confirmation of Promises.*

3. *It was an Evidence of Things not Seen.* Mark in the first place, that this sign which Gideon received, was

An Appeal to the Senses

Man is a compound being, and God deals with him as such. There is not a faculty, nor a gift with which man is endowed, to which God does not appeal in the great matter of salvation. This is an important consideration.

We are too apt to regard the atonement as a mere matter of faith. We believe it is something more: something greater, and something less. Gideon wished for a sign which his own hands could handle, and his own eyes could see. God granted him this sign – a sign, be it remembered, of greater things promised. Now it is just this sign, or this appeal to the senses, which appears in the atonement of our Lord. We lose much of the beauty of Scripture, we fail to appreciate the tender condescension of God, if we lose sight of this interesting and instructive truth.

The whole history of the atonement from the manger to the cross, from the tomb to the ascension, is an appeal to the senses. One voice throughout the whole life, and death, and resurrection of Jesus, seems to say, "Behold my hands and my feet, that it is I myself." (*Luke 24:39*). The beloved disciple, who leant on Jesus' bosom, realised the importance of this truth, when he said, in his first Epistle, "That which was from the beginning, which we have *heard*, which we have *seen* with our *eyes*, which we have *looked upon*, and our *hands* have *handled*, of the Word of Life."

Now, what does all this argue? Does it not show us that God hath given to his people the most tangible evidences, the most palpable and demonstrable proof, that He hath come down to visit them and deliver them? Were we all spirit, He might appeal to us *as spirit*. But as we are flesh and blood, gifted with hands and eyes, and endowed with animal senses, He appeals to all these, as to so many witnesses of His sovereign grace and amazing love. It is true that our own individual eyes have not seen Him, nor have our own ears heard Him speak, nor have our own hands handled his pierced side, but our fathers have had all these their senses satisfied – they saw, they heard, they handled, they believed, and they were saved.

And is not this enough? "Blessed are they who have not seen, and yet have believed." Do we not receive the testimony of credible witnesses upon other matters of by-gone fact? Through the senses of others, who lived ages ago, we embrace the facts recorded of ancient sages, of conquerors, of emperors. The great and the noble dead, live over again in our minds. We picture before our mental eye the histories of Cyrus, of Alexander, of Solon, of Demosthenes. We descend to later ages, and again we see the living pictures of Luther, and Melanchthon, of Calvin, and of Knox, of Cranmer, and of Latimer. We should be held incredulous and inexcusable, were we to throw aside all credible history, because our own eyes could not test its accuracy.

And what excuse shall we find in heaven, if we reject, or slight the testimony of others, on the matter of salvation? Where shall we be found in the day of final reckoning, if we accept not the sign which God has given us of his grace, and of his love? What if we be not saved? What if the heart be not given to Christ, and the Midianites within be not subdued? What excuse shall we have? Will not every sense and every faculty with which God has endowed our bodies, rise up and condemn us?

Will not the awful prophecy of Isaiah receive a fearful fulfilment in every such case, "This people's heart is waxed gross, and their *ears* are dull of hearing, and their *eyes* they have closed; lest at any time they should see with their *eyes*, and hear with their *ears*, and should understand with their heart, and should be converted, and I should heal them"?

But if, on the contrary, we embrace the sign which God has given us, and rely upon the wondrous facts of which they are signs, we then set to our seal that God is true. This is believing. This is acting faith in God. We trust God. We honour God.

Our senses harmonise with the faculties of our soul. The natural endowments of body and mind, accord with the graces of the Spirit. The whole creature is in unison with itself: and in unison with God. God's Word is *seen*, and *heard*, and *felt* to be true. We accept the witness of men as to facts. Through the witness of men, we receive the witness of God, which is greater. "For *this* is the witness of God which he hath testified of his Son … And *this* is the record that God hath given to us eternal life, and this life is in his Son. He that hath the Son, hath life; and he that hath not the Son of God hath not life." (*1 John 5:9-12*).

We notice, secondly, that this sign which the Lord gave unto Gideon, was

A Confirmation of Promises

The promises made to this mighty man of valour were of a two-fold nature, as emphatically expressed in *verse 16*, "The Lord said unto him, Surely I will be with thee, and thou shalt smite the Midianites as one man." The Lord's *presence*, and the Lord's *deliverance* were united. They always are so. They are inseparable. If the Lord be not with us, in vain shall we go forth against the Midianites, But "if the Lord be" with us, "none can prevail" against us.

Salvation, both present and eternal, is included in the promise, "I will be with thee." It is just this promise and blessing which are embodied in the name *Jesus*, which bears the same interpretation as "Immanuel," "God with us." Did not the Lord speak to Ahaz and bid him ask a sign, that His word is true – that He is with his people, and against their enemies? How significant were the words of God, when Ahaz shrunk from asking for a sign – "Therefore the Lord himself shall give you a sign; Behold, a virgin shall conceive, and bear a son, and shall call his name Immanuel." The birth of Jesus was God's great sign upon earth. No sign has equalled it, "either in the depths or in the height above." It surpasses all imagination of men, or angels. It proclaims to the wide universe, that God is with us, and against all our enemies. It is a double sign, and answers a double purpose. Angels shout "Hosannah!" and devils cry out, "Art thou come to torment us before the time?" This sign proclaims the fulfilment of all promises, and the accomplishment of all predictions. After this sign, there can be nothing too hard for the Lord. The Apostle wisely and logically argues from the greater to the less, when he triumphantly asks, "He that spared not his own Son, but delivered him up for us all, how shall he not with him also freely give us all things?" Were this sign but duly appreciated, were it seen in its infinite magnitude, all doubt would vanish, all fears would subside. God could give no greater sign that He loves the sinner. The sinner can imagine no greater. Every promise of pardon, of acceptance, of glory, is as dust in the balance compared with the eternal weight of evidence which this sign contains, of God's unfathomable love. Surely the weak may grow strong and valiant. The fearful may take courage. They need not fear a whole army of Midianitish opponents. In the glowing language of the Apostle, they may truly sing, "What shall we say to these things? If God be for us, who can be against us?"

But we see the confirmation of other predictions, and of other declarations, in the sign which God hath given, in the birth and death of Immanuel. We are amazed at the temerity of the unconverted and impenitent, who derive consolation from the wonders of Calvary! The sign of the cross is the most terrific sign which God could give, that He will in no wise clear the guilty. Fire arose out of the rock of Divine justice, enveloped and consumed sin, even though it were imputed to the Son of God! What if this fire find sin ingrained in the sinner! What if this fire of holy justice begin to play upon the conscience of the guilty! What if there be none to quench it! What if Dives cry aloud to father Abraham to send despised Lazarus to dip his finger in water, and cool his burning tongue! He that spared not his own Son *will not* – holy – awful – eternal justice – his own inflexible law – *could not* suffer him to spare the unpardoned sinner. Ah! what a sign is the sign of the cross! It is the believer's glory! It is the impenitent's terror! It is Satan's scourge! It is like the pillar of fire in the wilderness – all light on the one side; all darkness on the other side. That which is the sign of all salvation and glory to believers, is the sign of utter ruin and misery to unbelievers. The sign of the cross speaks in language prophetic of coming doom – "The sinners in Zion are afraid; fearfulness hath surprised the hypocrites. Who among us shall dwell with the devouring fire? Who among us shall dwell with everlasting burnings?" (*Isaiah 33:14*).

The sign vouchsafed to Gideon was also

An Evidence of Things Not Seen

It was an appeal to sense to strengthen faith. Gideon was "a mighty man of valour," but his faith was now weak. He seemed almost to doubt the truth of the miracles of old, because no miracles were now wrought for the deliverance of Israel. Gideon said unto the angel, in answer to his salutation, "The Lord is with thee" – "Oh my Lord, *if* the Lord *be* with us, why then is all this befallen us? And where be all his miracles which our fathers told us of?" And then, when the Lord looked upon Gideon, and said, "Go in this thy might, and thou shalt save Israel," his faith faltered, and, in doubt of his success, he said, "Oh my Lord, wherewith shall *I* save Israel? Behold my family is poor in Manasseh, and I am the least in my father's house." Gideon took a gloomy view of Israel's condition. He could see no help for them, no strength in his own arm, no influence from his own social or political *status*. He was a poor man, and insignificant, and what could *he* do? Had the angel appeared to one of the rich men in Manasseh, had he come even to the head of his own family, there might have been some hope. The combination of wealth and family influence might possibly unite the bands of Israel, and thus defeat the Midianites! Thus Gideon seemed to reason, and to take counsel of flesh and blood for a season. But, at length, the true secret of the strength of this man of valour began to show itself. He seemed to awaken suddenly to a consciousness that He was no mere man, who had thus accosted him under the oak in Ophrah. What if He were an angel! What if it were even He who had delivered Israel from Egypt! *Whose look* was *that* which so penetrated his inmost soul? *Whose voice* which said, "Have not *I* sent thee?" Faith arose from the ashes of doubt. He will put the matter to a test. If it *be* the Lord, he will ask for some satisfactory proof of the fact – "And he said unto him, If now I have found grace in thy sight, then show me a sign that *thou* talkest with me."

That sign, so wondrously given, was an evidence to Gideon of things not seen. It proved to him that He who appeared as a man, "under the oak which was in Ophrah" was none other than the Angel of the Lord – even the Angel of the everlasting covenant! It proved, moreover, that Gideon was called of God to deliver Israel. Oh that he might succeed in the attempt! He had no riches, no name, no influence, no soldiers; but no matter, the Lord was indeed "with him," and that was enough. He would now act up to the title which the Lord had given him, as a "mighty man of valour," and Israel shall be delivered, by "the sword of the Lord and of Gideon."

"Now faith is the substance of things hoped for, the evidence of things not seen. For by it the elders obtained a good report ... By faith the walls of Jericho fell down ... by faith the harlot Rahab perished not ... And what shall I more say? for the time would fail me to tell of Gideon, and of Barak, and of Samson, and of Jephthae; of David also, and Samuel, and of the prophets: who through faith subdued kingdoms, wrought righteousness, obtained promises, stopped the mouths of lions, quenched the violence of fire, escaped the edge of the sword, out of weakness were made strong, waxed valiant in fight, turned to flight the armies of the aliens." (*Hebrews 11:1, 2, 30-34*).

Now it is just this faith in an unseen presence, and in an unfelt power, which saves the soul from spiritual Midianites. We have no strength for the battle – no might – no sufficiency. He who relies upon an arm of flesh leans upon a broken reed. How often have we realised the weakness of all human power. "We wrestle not against flesh and blood." Divine power alone is equal to cope with Satanic might. The sinner who wars against his sins, his lusts, his evil passions, his corrupt nature, in his own strength, soon proves his folly and his weakness. Satan laughs all his feeble efforts to scorn. As well attempt to bind Satan by firm resolves in human might, as to bind Samson with green withs. As regards all spiritual conquests, one word should at once check the vain conceit of the sinner, and strengthen the faith of the child of God – "Not by might, nor by power, but by my Spirit, saith the Lord of hosts."

Do you look for any *sign* that the Lord is with you – that He will deliver you, and make you victorious over all your enemies? Behold that sign upon the hard rock of Calvary! Behold it in that mysterious fire which arose therefrom! Behold it in the utter consumption of the sacrifice! Behold it in the ascent of the Lord himself, from off the altar, to his throne of glory! What further sign can you need?

This sign accepted, God's plan of deliverance rested upon, Jesus embraced by living faith, as "the wisdom of God, and the power of God" – all grace, all victory, all salvation, are yours. The sign is yours that God himself talketh with you on earth, as friend talketh with friend; and yours may be the joyful and blessed assurance that, when He appeareth again, He will receive you unto Himself, that "where He is, there you may be also," and that for ever.

But why not accept the sign of the cross? Why avert the eye from the beams of the Sun of Righteousness whose melting rays are gathered together in this one burning focus? What, is sin so sweet, so precious, that you tremble lest it be discovered, and be made to appear dark, hideous, satanic, in the light of the cross? Or, is it so, that you would rather perish than enter heaven with the right eye plucked out, or with the right hand cut off? "Ah! no; it is not so with *me*," cries out the sinner, trembling in his sins. "Gladly would I look – thankfully would I rend off this my right hand, if, by so doing, pardon of my sins were sealed to my conscience, and assurance of salvation were to enter my soul; but that sign, so clear, so tangible to others, so full of hope and immortality to others, only proves to me that God is of purer eyes than to behold iniquity in me."

We ask, Whence this inference? We demand, Whence this perversion of the sign of the cross? We inquire, *Whence* is that logic, which would argue *death*, from God's revelation, and sign of *life?* Whence comes that dark, foul, and God-dishonouring doubt, which calls in question the most overwhelming, most convincing, and most melting sign of love, and reads therein naught but an evidence of hate? Whose lie against God's sign is this? What is that which makes God a liar? Ah! tremble, O sinner, that thou hast not trembled more! Thou hast *yet* to learn the deep, dark depravity of thine heart of unbelief, which listens to the whispers of the enemy of God and man, and loves them too! Awake! awake! Thou art drinking in poison from the lips of Satan. Awake! His foul hand darkens thine eyes; thou hast not yet obtained a clear view of the cross! Listen to the deceiver no longer. Up; turn your eye to Jesus. Venture all upon Him. Come to Him at once. Come as you are. Come, doubting, for faith. Come, weak, for strength. Come, blind, for light. Come, lost, to be saved. Come at once – come now – and He will say to you, "Be not faithless, but believe, – that it is I myself, who bled for thee on the cross, and that now appeareth unto thee, as the God of thy salvation." This will be his gracious answer, when thou shalt approach Him, and pray, "Show me a *sign* that thou talkest with me."

3
Jehovah-Shalom

"Then Gideon built an altar there unto the Lord, and called it
Jehovah-Shalom." ["*The Lord send peace*"] (*Judges 6:24*)

"Who feels the worth of peace? He who has lost
  Its gladdening light when threatening clouds are nigh;
He who has viewed the agony it cost
  The Saviour of mankind that peace to buy.

"'My peace I give,' – what wondrous words are those
  Who knows their import, and their full increase?
None ever will, till this poor life shall close,
  And heaven reveals full, perfect, deathless peace!"

MEMORIAL altars were of ancient date. Long had the custom
of erecting them prevailed. Abraham, "the father of the
faithful," reared his memorial altar upon Moriah's Mount, when the
Lord spared his beloved Isaac, and revealed Himself unto him, and
"he called the name of the place Jehovah-jireh," that is, the Lord "will
see," or "provide."

Jacob, too, took the stony pillow on which his head had lain, when
visions of heaven were granted unto him, and he consecrated it with
oil, and called the place Bethel, that is, "the house of God," and on
that spot, by Divine command, he afterwards reared an altar.

Moses, the man of God, dedicated a memorial altar unto the Lord,
in remembrance of the victory over Amalek, and called it "Jehovah-
nissi," that is, "the Lord my banner."

And now, we read of Gideon, "the mighty man of valour," building his altar unto the Lord, founded upon a rock, as a memorial of
the angel's visit, who appeared unto him under the oak which was in

Ophrah, and of his having talked with Him face to face, and of his life being spared according to the word of the Lord. Appropriately did he make choice of the name by which he designated this altar. He called it "Jehovah-shalom," that is, "The Lord send peace." Great had been his fears *for himself* – that he should die, – but he was assured by the Lord that he should live, and he accepted and embraced the promise of life, and said, "Jehovah-shalom." Great too, were his fears *for his beloved country* – war, oppression, and bloodshed were before his eyes – but the Lord promised that he should deliver Israel and restore peace to her borders, and he trusted in the words uttered, and the sign given by the Lord, and in token of his faith and gratitude erected his altar, and called it, "Jehovah-shalom."

There is much deep instruction here. Let us strive to understand the full depth of Gideon's meaning.

Let us approach the subject in order, and notice: 1. *Gideon's fear.* 2. *Gideon's fear removed.* 3. *Gideon's altar.* Each of these points invites distinct and clear elucidation.

Gideon's Fear

"When Gideon perceived that he was an angel of the Lord, Gideon said, Alas, O Lord God! for because I have seen an angel of the Lord face to face."

Gideon's fear was *traditional.* It was a commonly-received opinion that no man could receive a direct manifestation from heaven, and live. Jacob was amazed when his life was spared, after he had wrestled with the unknown man, until break of day; and he called the name of the place Peniel, that is, "the face of God;" "for I have seen God face to face, and my life is preserved."

Whence arose this tradition? What was the cause of this fear? Adam, when he walked in the cool of eventide, amid the bowers of a sinless Paradise, had no such fear. God talked with him face to face, in open vision, and *he* had no fear of death. No threat of instant death upon such manifestation of God had ever been heard by Jacob, nor uttered by the lips of Jehovah. The very opposite inference might have been drawn from such marvellous condescension on the part of God. Will God indeed revisit this earth, from which sin would have banished Him; will He, indeed, hold personal converse with sinners, whose proud and rebellious hearts have often said, "Who is Lord over us?" If, therefore, He come, surely He must come in peace, and mercy, and love, and there is hope of life and glory! Whence, then, this fear, this dread apprehension of instant death at His presence?

Let Peter tell us. Having toiled all night in fishing, and having caught nothing, at the word of One who stood on the margin of the lake, he let down his net again, and enclosed so great a draught of fishes, that his net brake. Peter at once became sensible of the Divine presence. He beheld One greater than the son of Mary, in Him who had thus spoken, and thus commanded the fishes of the sea. "He fell down at Jesus' knees, saying, Depart from me, for I am a sinful man, O Lord."

The presence of the Lord awoke in Peter's heart a deep and overwhelming sense of sin. He felt there was such an awful and inexpressible contrast between his sinfulness and the Lord's holiness, that he could endure the manifestation no longer. Hence, he gave vent to the full impulse of his astonished soul, "Depart from me; for I am a sinful man, O Lord."

Similar were the feelings of Jacob, of Gideon, and of others. Ever since the fall of Adam in Paradise, man has ever shunned, and dreaded, the immediate presence of Jehovah. Adam and Eve hid themselves from God, behind the trees in the garden. And man's first thought from that time forth has been to follow the example of our first parents, whenever God has revealed himself from heaven.

Alas, what has sin done! It makes man dread the presence of his Maker! It makes him shun intercourse with God! It makes him cry out in alarm, "Depart from me," when the only Saviour appeareth on his behalf. It makes Gideon tremble, and cry aloud in terror, "Alas, O Lord God!" after the Lord God had graciously assured him, "Surely I will be with thee."

If the *righteous* thus fear, and thus tremble, when the Lord revealeth himself unto them in love and peace, "where shall the ungodly and the sinner appear," when He cometh forth from his place, and sweareth that He will by no means clear the guilty?

Why do not unpardoned and unsanctified sinners tremble for themselves, and dread entering into the presence of God? How comes it to pass that they live so merrily, and that there are no bands in their death? Are righteous and holy men all deceived? Are they terrified and affrighted at old wives' fables, and at mere phantoms? Some men have ever *thought so*. Some have impiously *said so*. The sons-in-law of

Lot joined all Sodom and Gomorrah in declaring that they knew it to be so. Even Lot's wife had some doubts on the point. But others "*believe*," and yet, unlike those who realise the fact, do not "*tremble*." How comes it to pass, we ask, that men who profess their faith in the Bible, and yet live in the world, and for the world – who banish God as much as possible from their thoughts – whose lives proclaim them totally unfit for the presence of the pure and holy in heaven – how is it, that *they* can "rush in where angels fear to tread"? There can be but one answer. We need no deep learning, no philosophic researches to find it out. There is one simple cause for the whole evil, – an evil so great and so awful that angels marvel at the sight, and devils stand amazed at the success of their own devices; – and this one cause is, "They are *hardened* through the *deceitfulness* of sin." They are duped and hardened by sin. "Thou shalt not surely die," is the deceitful lie which the Serpent still whispers in the ears of the children of Eve. And as long as sin is loved, and Satan's whispers are cherished, so long will the heart remain hardened, and no terror will awaken to a true sense of danger, until with Dives, the eyes be lifted up in hell, and the soul cry out in agony and despair, "Alas, O Lord God!"

And now, behold

Gideon's Fear Removed

There was but ONE who could remove the fear which his own presence had imparted. And it was He who graciously subdued the terror of this man of God, and said, "Peace be unto thee; fear not, thou shalt not die."

There was more than a mere salutation in those few words, "Peace be unto thee." Gideon would never have found heart to have built up his memorial altar, or called it "Jehovah-shalom," if peace itself had not entered his heart, when those words entered his ears. He who pronounced the words, bestowed the blessing.

Fear vanished, as soon as peace appeared with her olive branch. "Thou shalt not die," was an assurance which found a deep response in Gideon's encouraged heart.

His peace was the effect, and assurance of life. Had any doubt of life remained, fear would have reigned, and peace would have departed. We see, then, that the Lord's gracious presence, as revealed to Gideon, was a blessed token of peace, that his fears were groundless, and that his life was in safe custody.

You will not fail to observe, that it was upon the strength of the assurance thus given to this trembling, and yet mighty man of valour, that he built an altar there, and called it "Jehovah-shalom."

And what is that which now quells the fears of the trembling sinner? What is that which assures him of peace, takes away his alarms, and imparts to his soul holy confidence that he shall not die? This altar, Jehovah-shalom, is an altar which many a grateful, loving heart has built up high above all the storms and tempests of life, and all the dread fears of death. And what has done all this? Whence the joy of saints? Whence the peace which passeth all understanding? Whence the almost angelic smile which plays upon the face of Stephen as he looks up into heaven, and breathes forth his ransomed soul, in the simple words, "Lord Jesus, receive my spirit"? Whence that panting desire to depart, and be with Christ, which so illumines the dying saint, that death himself withdraws his hand at the sight? Does the Lord's presence alone accomplish all this? What said alarmed Peter? – "Depart from me, O Lord!" What cried out terrified Manoah? – "We shall surely die, because we have seen God." What exclaimed Gideon? – "Alas, O Lord God! for because I have seen an angel of the Lord face to face." The presence of the Lord does not of itself impart either life, or peace. Jesus hung between two thieves. They both saw him. They both heard him. They both beheld his wondrous death. But one only entered Paradise. Ah, no! it is not the mere presence of the Lord which gives peace to the heart, and life to the soul. The Lord was as often near to Judas, as He was to John.

What, then, we ask again, was that which built up Gideon's altar, "Jehovah-shalom"? What is that which opens the heart to peace, and assures the soul of endless life? There is but one grand means – there is but one grand channel. It is not far off. You need take no long and perilous journey to obtain it. "Say not in thine heart, who shall bring Christ down from above, or who shall descend into the deep, that is, to bring up Christ again from the dead. But what saith the Lord? The Word is nigh thee, even in thy mouth, and in thy heart, that is, the Word of faith, which we preach: That if thou wilt confess with thy mouth the Lord Jesus, and shalt believe in thine heart that God hath raised him from the dead, thou shalt be saved. For with the heart man believeth unto righteousness; and with the mouth confession is made unto salvation."

The pure and simple word of God was that which Gideon believed. It was that alone, which, by the Holy Spirit's application, imparted peace, and assured his soul of life. And this is still, and ever will be, God's method of bringing peace and salvation to sinners. God's presence alone does but alarm and terrify. We cannot look upon a holy God, and not fear.

Our sins are too many, and too great, to suffer us to bear the presence of Jehovah. But let us hear his voice of love speaking peace; let us but hear Him say, "There is peace made for thee, poor trembling sinner, in the blood of the Lamb; Jesus has borne away all thy transgressions; My holy law is perfectly, and for ever satisfied – fear not; He has died on yonder hard rock of justice in thy stead; thou shalt not die, but live; and live in Him, and live by Him for ever." Why, then, no wonder that the altar of gratitude is erected in the believing heart, and that we call it "Jehovah-shalom."

But if men turn a deaf ear to this word of the Gospel; if they stand trembling or hardened in the presence of God; alike unfit to live or to die – if they listen to the voice of gain or pleasure; if they turn a more ready ear to the sounds of sin or temptation, than they do to the words of the Most High – is it any wonder that they are strangers to peace? What have *they* to do with peace, as long as they reject, or neglect the word of the Prince of Peace? Would that I were gifted with words which would startle them to a sense of their danger. Would that the voice of the charmer could charm more wisely, that deaf ears might be broken open. But I fear, and fear horribly, for the sinners that are at ease in Zion. What if they shun the Word of the living God now? What if they close up His book, and take up the newspaper, the novel, the history, the latest work on science, or philosophy now? What if the Bible be closed now, because it does not, and no torturing will ever make it, speak peace to any man who lives in his sins? What if all this be true, and far more also? How will these men listen to the voice of the same God; with what feelings will they prepare themselves to hear his Word, when his voice shall rend the mountains, and call forth the dead from their graves?

And now, mark

Gideon's Altar

Observe its significant *name*. He called it Jehovah-shalom, that is, "*The Lord send peace.*" This altar was a memorial of *three* things – of

Gideon's *faith*, and *hope*, and *gratitude*. For a moment look at it in this three-fold light.

1. *What a memorial of Gideon's faith* was it! As soon as the Lord had spoken the words of promise, Gideon raised his altar, not only in remembrance of the promise, but as an evidence that he trusted in it.

The greatest act of man towards God is faith – a reception of his Word, and a reliance upon it. All things are possible to him that believeth. "What shall we do," said the Jews to Jesus, "that we might work the works of God?" A large and important question this! How variously would men answer it! One would say, the work of God is *this* great act, and another would say, it is *that*. But Jesus at once put his finger upon the spring of all good actions, and said, "This is the work of God, that ye *believe* on him whom he hath sent." Gideon thus believed, and believing, peace entered his heart: his hand grasped the sword, and his stout arm overthrew the altar of Baal, and smote down the hosts of the Midianites.

"Who is he that overcometh the world?" asks the Apostle John. And many have asked the same question before, and since, his day. But there is only one answer to it. And that is an answer which every conqueror realises: "He that believeth that Jesus is the Son of God."

2. This altar was, moreover, *a memorial of Gideon's hope.*

Gideon was called by God to deliver Israel. He had no sufficiency for the enterprise. He felt this. "Wherewith shall I save Israel?" was the inquiry of his fear. "Behold, my family is poor in Manasseh, and I am the least in my father's house." I can do nothing, he seemed to think; it is of no use for the Lord to call me to do this great work.

But no sooner had the Lord displayed his power upon that wondrous rock, and assured Gideon that he should not die, but live, than his faith and hope arose, and he was ready for any dangerous enterprise to which he might be called, and therefore he built an altar in token of the hope which now filled his heart, and called it "Jehovah-shalom" – "The Lord send peace."

"Hope maketh not ashamed!" How sweet, how precious is the Christian's hope. It is no vain wish, or mere fervent desire of the mind. It is a grace of the Holy Spirit which He alone kindles in the heart. It is the crowning grace of all. The armour of the Christian is completed, and adorned, by the pluming "helmet of the hope of salvation." Hope is the younger sister of faith. She is more joyful, more buoyant than faith. She is called "lively hope." But she has no life apart from faith. She lives in the warm bosom of faith. Faith carries her in her arms. Faith raises her high in her own chariot. If faith overcomes the world, hope spreads her wings, and soars to heaven. "Jehovah-shalom" is the language of hope. "The Lord *has* sent peace" – "the Lord *will* send peace." Hope is as an anchor of the soul, which faith casts within the veil, and there she stays the soul with such strong consolation, that no storm nor tempest can destroy the peace, and comfort, and joy which she imparts.

Ah! this would be a dreary world without hope! When earthly hope vanishes, and despair enters the heart, no mere human, no extraneous help, will raise a man above himself. And what is the soul without hope – this faith-imparted, faith-nourished hope? Why are not Christians more holy, more devoted to God, more cheerful in his service? Is it not because hope is suffered to pine away almost to death? Talk of the joyfulness of hope – speak of the full assurance of hope – declare that hope is the crowning grace of the Spirit – tell them of the sure and steadfast anchor of hope – unfold the promise and oath of God who holds that anchor within the veil, and Christian men imagine that you are speaking of high mountains of Christian experience, which they are never expected to climb! Alas! it is no wonder that doubts, and fears, and spiritual weaknesses so much abound, when God's children love to dwell, and are contented to live, in the low and damp atmosphere of the theories of men, rather than ascend the high rock of God's pure Word.

And if true believers – real Christians – God's own children – need more of this "hope which maketh not ashamed" – if their faith at times fails to bring joy and peace in believing – what are we to say, what are we to think of some, who are living "without God, and without hope in the world"? I say to them, in all heartfelt sincerity: blind *credulity* you have *much*, but true *faith* you have *none*. Hopes and wishes, unsolid, intangible, "as the baseless fabric of a dream," you have many: but hope built upon the firm rock of unchangeable truth, you have none. Joy it may be, and pleasure, too, you think you have. We will not doubt it. We know full well *what* it is! The butterfly has pleasure as it dances in the beams of the midday sun. The moth has pleasure as it flits entranced around the candle. But is *this happiness?* – happiness which becomes a never-dying soul? Are the hopes which are bounded by the playthings of a day, worthy of the immortal nature of one who was made in the image of God? Ah! folly! Ah! madness! to talk of hope which will die out with the wear and tear of this earthly tabernacle. Such a hope is to him who wears it, no fit helmet for the soul, but a cap of folly! *Who* would venture into eternity with such a helmet on as *this?*

But let living faith in the crucified and risen Jesus live in the heart; let this faith cherish hope, and that hope will stand upon the high rock of eternity, erect, sublime, and glorious, and amid the crash of the universe, shout aloud, "Jehovah-shalom" – The Lord send peace.

3. Gideon's altar was, lastly, a *memorial of his gratitude.*

He could never look upon that altar without recalling to his mind the wonders of the past. Placing his hand upon it he would say, "This is the hallowed spot where the angel Jehovah visited me – here He displayed His gracious presence unto me – here He spared my life – here He promised to be with me – here He declared that I should deliver Israel from her enemies. O altar! be thou an abiding witness, on this high rock, that the Word of the living God is faithful and true, and that not one jot nor one tittle of all that God has spoken, will ever fall to the ground. O altar! thy name shall be for ever called, Jehovah-shalom."

Thus many a memorial of gratitude has been raised by pious and loving hearts. "What shall I render unto the Lord for all his benefits towards me?" was David's grateful inquiry. Gratitude welled up in Jacob's full heart at Bethel, when he "vowed a vow, saying, If God will be with me, and will keep me in this way that I go, and will give me bread to eat, and raiment to put on, so that I come again in peace; then shall the Lord be my God: and this stone which I have set for a pillar, shall be God's house: and of all that thou shalt give me, I will surely give the tenth unto thee." "Ye are not your own," saith the Apostle Paul, "for ye are bought with a price." Ah! let this purchase be valued – let this price be estimated – let imagination attempt to conceive its infinite magnitude, and endless consequences, and then ask, What memorial can be commensurate with that deep sense of fervent love, and gratitude, which should overflow the heart? Surely whatever be the subsequent acts of the soul – however great, however noble be the sentiments and deeds of grateful love, which shall *plan* great things, and *dare* great things, and *accomplish* great things for the Lord, we shall all agree that the very *first* thing the sinner has to do, and which if he *does not*, it is because he has neither part nor lot in the matter of salvation, is, to obey the exhortation of the Apostle, "I beseech you, therefore, brethren, by the mercies of God, that ye *present your bodies a living sacrifice*, holy, acceptable unto God, which is your reasonable service."

4

The Valorous Assault

"Will ye plead for Baal? will ye save him? he that will plead for
him, let him be put to death whilst it is yet morning: if he be
a god, let him plead for himself, because one hath cast down
his altar." (*Judges 6:31*)

"Soldier, go – but not to claim
  Mouldering spoils of earth-born treasure,
Not to build a vaunting name,
  Not to dwell in tents of pleasure.
Dream not that the way is smooth,
  Hope not that the thorns are roses;
Turn no wishful eye of youth,
  Where the sunny beam reposes;
  Thou hast sterner work to do,
  Hosts to cut thy passage through
Close behind thee gulfs are burning –
Forward! – there is no returning."

WE have here a question of life or death. The penalty of idolatry
in Israel was death. *Who* was the guilty one? Gideon who
pleaded for Jehovah, or the Israelite who pleaded for Baal?

Who was the true God in Israel? Jehovah, or Baal? This was the
real question at issue.

It was some time, however, before the religious controversy was
thus narrowed. Israel had attempted to compromise matters. They
had no wish to become bigots. They wanted men to follow their own
religious opinions without let or hindrance. They were opposed, or
thought they were opposed, to all intolerance. In fact, they were so
liberal in their ideas of religious liberty, that they had no objection to

two gods. They urged that this liberty of conscience would satisfy all parties, and offend none. As long as there were no hypocrites, as long as men were sincere in their religion, and were good neighbours and good citizens; what did it matter what religious creed they held? If Gideon wished to worship the God of his fathers, and him only; by all means let him do so. But *why* should *he* interfere with the worship and religious opinions of others? Why should *he* be allowed to be a troubler in Israel? Such a bigot and self-religious Pharisee as *he;* such a narrow-minded and intolerant exclusionist as *he*, is not fit to live upon earth! He opposes better, and older, and wiser men than himself. He sets himself up against even his own father, and his father's house! Away with him! He is unworthy of the age! He is only fit to live in the dark ages of Mosaic tyranny! His good and liberal-minded father will surely disown him as his son, and denounce him as worthy of death! "Joash, bring out thy son that he may die!"

Such is a picture of religion in Israel 1200 years BC. That picture, although so old, looks as fresh as ever – as fresh as life – in the present age of the Christian era. The canvas lives and breathes. A master's hand is here, as in other parts of this truth-telling Book. When *Romans 1* was first read to some of the native tribes of Africa, they could scarcely be persuaded that the missionary had not just written it, so graphically descriptive was it of their own state.

Let us look, then, a little closer at the narrative before us. May the Holy Spirit help us to learn the Divine lesson which it contains! If He bless us we shall hear, mark, and learn to profit; but, if He bless not, our eyes will see not, our ears will hear not, our hearts will understand not.

Two leading points are before us: 1. *God's Command.* 2. *Gideon's Obedience.* Rich are the lessons to be drawn from both of these heads.

God's Command to Gideon

He did not throw down Baal's altar at the suggestion of his own mind. He was obeying a mightier influence than his own feelings. He did not act upon his own authority. He was like Peter and John in after ages, who obeyed God rather than man. The same night in which he had offered a meat offering upon the rock, out of which the wondrous fire arose, the Lord said unto him, "Take thy father's young bullock, even the second bullock of seven years old, and throw down the altar of Baal, that thy father hath, and cut down the grove that is by it: and build an altar unto the Lord thy God upon the top of this rock, in the ordered place, and take the second bullock, and offer a burnt sacrifice with the wood of the grove which thou shalt cut down."

You will observe that Gideon was commanded to do three things:

- He was to throw down the altar of Baal.
- He was to cut down Baal's grove.
- He was to build a new altar unto the Lord.

Carefully examine these *three* duties, and you will at once see their bearing upon ourselves.

1. Gideon is commanded *to destroy the altar of Baal.*

A great work was before this "mighty man of valour." He was chosen to be Israel's deliverer from her enemies. But before the Midianites can be expelled, the altar of Baal must be thrown down. Before Jehovah's altar can be built, the altar of Baal must be destroyed. There can be no interchange of altars – no compromise between God and Baal. "God *or* Baal" – not "God *and* Baal" – was the point to be settled, before any deliverance could be expected.

Now, throw New Testament light upon this, and what do we learn? The lesson is trumpet-tongued. The lips of the Lord Jesus speak, and his voice declareth, "No man can serve two masters. He that is not with me is against me. Ye cannot serve God and mammon." No compromise – no halting between two opinions – is the language of the command. God hates a divided heart. He will not endure two altars. He will give no deliverance as long as Baal's altar stands. It must come down. Not a stone of it must be left. He will not give deliverance from sin, and death, and hell, as long as any compromise is attempted. No sacrifice however costly, is, or can be, accepted, which is offered upon the polluted altar of man's corrupt heart. A new altar must be built up – an altar of God's workmanship – *of* God, and *for* God, – *that* is the only altar which will sanctify an acceptable gift. Any attempt to worship at Jehovah's altar on one day in seven, and to worship at the altar of Baal, or Mammon, on the other six days in the week, is not only vain, but suicidal. God will have a new heart, and a whole heart, or none. Baal's altar must be thrown down. No matter who worships before it – no matter who pleads for it – relatives, neighbours, countrymen, moral men, or immoral, down, and down to the ground, it must come. Deliverance from the enemy succeeds through destruction of the enemy's altar. Half measures are ruinous. "What fellowship hath righteousness with unrighteousness? And what communion hath light with darkness? And what concord hath Christ with Belial? And what part hath he that believeth with an infidel? And what agreement hath the temple of God with idols?"

Gideon's work was *material.* An arm of flesh could, and did throw down the altar of Baal. He, with his ten servants, was equal to the enterprise.

But "*we* wrestle *not against flesh and blood.*" It is not a material altar which has to be overthrown in our heart. We wrestle "against principalities, and powers, and spiritual wickedness in high places." Satan laughs to scorn all attempts of human power to overthrow him. "A stronger than the strong man armed," must enter upon the work, and do this. And He is ever ready to help the helpless. The Holy Spirit is mighty to overthrow Baal's altar, and to build up Jehovah's in the sinner's heart. Call Him in, and out of weakness you will be made strong, and so great will be the transformation of your heart and life, that many will marvel at the change, and say, "Who hath done this thing?"

2. The next thing Gideon was commanded to do, was to *cut down Baal's grove*, and make it fuel for the altar of God.

Groves were planted near the altars of the false gods, not only in honour of the idols, but for the worst of heathen practices. Now Baal's grove must not stand, after Baal's altar has been thrown down.

Need we an interpreter here? It is not enough to overthrow the idol in the heart, but everything planted in honour of that idol, everything that helped his worship, everything that tempted the heart to idolatry, must be cut down, and burnt. Groves were not idolatrous – there was no harm in them – but they were occasions of sin. How many had been ruined and ruined for ever, under the foliage of those groves. Perversion of nature's growth to the dishonour of nature's God! Many would plead for the harmless trees, who would condemn both Baal and his idolatrous worship. But God knows the heart of the sinner better than he knows it himself: and therefore He says, "Cut down the grove." Cut down the occasion of sin. Touch not, taste not, handle not that which causes men to perish with the using. Avoid the spot, shun the places where Satan's seat is, – where he has reigned, and souls have perished, where once you sought sinful pleasure. Ah! cut it down – wipe out its memory from your heart.

Do more than this! God commanded Gideon to "offer a burnt sacrifice with the wood of the grove." This was turning the idolatrous grove to a good purpose. Let there be no waste – no useless destruction. Turn every creature of God, hitherto abused, to the service of God. Place every stick you cut down upon the altar of your God. Offer it to Him. Money, health, time, influence, example, all, once expended for Baal, now let them all be as fuel for the altar of God. The Apostle meant nothing less than this, when he wrote to the Roman Christians, and said: "As ye have yielded your members servants to uncleanness, and to iniquity unto iniquity: *even so now* yield your members servants to righteousness unto holiness." Cut down the whole grove, and apply it to the service of God. Let every faculty and energy of body, and mind, and soul, once employed in serving the world, the flesh, and the devil, be now consecrated to a holy purpose. Give the whole grove to God. Let it burn upon His altar. You cannot spare the grove, if you throw down the idolatrous altar. Lot's wife attempted to spare the grove, after she had thrown down the altar in Sodom. But the grove in her heart was her destruction. Half measures are ruinous. "The axe *must be* laid unto the root of the trees: therefore every tree which bringeth not forth good fruit, *must be* hewn down, and cast into the fire."

3. The third thing God commanded Gideon to do, was to *build an altar unto the Lord his God.*

But *where* was this altar to be reared? Was it to stand on the spot whereon Baal's altar stood? No! the place is polluted. On no unhallowed spot must this altar be raised. Build it, said the Lord, "upon the top of this rock, in the ordered place." Gideon must build it upon the rock already consecrated, by the wondrous doings thereon of the angel of the covenant. Out of that rock rose up fire which consumed Gideon's offering. It was upon *that* rock that Gideon perceived that he had seen this angel face to face. It was whilst he stood upon that rock, that the Lord had said unto him, "Peace be unto thee; fear not: thou shalt not die."

How significant this command, "Build an altar unto the Lord thy God upon the top of *this rock*." On that rock I have appeared to thee in mercy – on that rock I have accepted thee – on that rock I have

41

declared to thee peace and life. What rock answers to this rock in the Christian's faith? May we not say of this rock, what Paul said of the smitten rock in the wilderness, "That rock was Christ." He is indeed both altar and rock – yea, He is Himself the sacrifice. Standing on Him alone as our Rock, we ever hear the sweet words, "Peace be unto thee; fear not: thou shalt not die." He only is the true rock – higher than we – far above the flood which sweeps the impenitent into the depths of woe. He, too, only is the Rock on which we can with safety place the altar of our hearts. The old foundation will not do – it is polluted – it is defiling. No altar, no sacrifice will God accept if it be offered upon the site of Baal's altar.

"Behold, I make all things new" – this is our hope to come. This must be the rule of our faith and practice now. The old foundation is corrupt, defiled, polluting. We must have a new rock – a new heart – a new life – and ourselves be made new creatures in Christ; old things must pass away, and all things must become new. The change must be radical. There must be no amalgamation of God's altar with Baal's. Not a stone of Baal's altar must be used. Pull down his altar – scatter its stones to the four winds – cut down his grove – burn the wood – burn it to cinders upon the altar of the Lord – but the altar itself must be new, and upon this Rock *only* must it be built. Compromise there can be none. Dear Reader, upon what rock are you building your hopes? Can you say, "I have thrown down the altar of Baal; I have cut down his grove, and burnt all the timber; and now I am resting all my salvation upon the atonement and finished work of Christ"? If thus you are building, peace be unto you; fear not: you shall not die. "Upon this rock Christ builds his Church, and the gates of hell shall not prevail against it."

Gideon's Obedience

It was a perilous duty which this man of God had to perform. To go and fight against Midian was far easier, and required less grace, than to fight against Baal, and the religious faith of his countrymen. Many a "mighty man of valour" has found it harder work to take up the cross of Christ, and fight against sin, than to draw the two-edged sword, and fight against the enemy in the open field of battle. But, as we go on, we shall see more and more to admire, in the noble character of Gideon.

1. His obedience was *prompt*. He seems to have begun his perilous work on the very night in which God had given him the command. *Verse 27* records his prompt obedience – "Then Gideon took ten men of his servants, and did as the Lord had said unto him." He "conferred not with flesh and blood." He did not give himself time to take counsel of his fears. He did it *by night*, lest he should be opposed and hindered. He had no fear on account of detection. He must have known that his deed would be proclaimed over the whole nation. His aim was to do the work out of hand, and leave the consequences with God. Duty was his, events were God's.

Noble example! Half the shipwrecks of faith would be escaped were it followed. Procrastination is the bane of true godliness. It is the thin end of the wedge. It is a bait to the tempter. How often a good and noble resolution, which, if acted upon and followed up, would have ended in salvation, had not flesh and blood been conferred with. Paul preached. Felix heard him, and Felix trembled! Oh! what a prospect began to open before the Roman Governor! Who knows but angels will rejoice over his conversion and salvation! But, no! He procrastinated. Foolish man, he waited for "*a more* convenient season"! A more convenient season than when an apostle preached to him! Conscience spoke to him, the Spirit strove with him! A more convenient season! Alas! what *right* had he to expect it? It never came!

Why do so many hearers of the Gospel perish? It is easy to resolve their ruin into the sovereignty of God. But is it wise, is it just to do so? Does God himself do so? Does He not say, "How long, ye simple ones, will ye love simplicity? And the scorners delight in their scorning, and fools hate knowledge? Turn you at my reproof: behold, I will pour out my Spirit unto you, I will make known my words unto you. Because I have called, and ye refused; I have stretched out my hand, and no man regarded … I also will laugh at your calamity: I will mock when your fear cometh." Whence comes this ruin of the soul? Is it intentional? Are men so simple as deliberately to choose death rather than life? Do they mean to lie down in their sins for ever? No! They have no such intention. Baal's altar is to come down one of these days! But they will wait for "a more convenient season." They do not wish to be in too great a hurry. A few matters have to be settled with Baal first, before they will raise the axe, and give the fatal blow to his altar. The flames have burst out in the house, the smoke has entered his chamber, but the sluggard turns upon his bed once more, and pleads for a little more slumber, and a little more sleep. An enemy whispers in his ear, "No immediate danger yet. Sleep on, sleep on, sleep on; take your rest." And he sleeps, and sleeps, and sleeps again, until some terrible crash arouses him, and he awakes in the fire that cannot be quenched.

2. We observe, however, that Gideon's obedience was *attended with personal danger.*

He needed courage, and strong faith. Doubtless he sought for grace equal to that night of danger, whence alone all strength cometh. The followers of Baal – the men of the city – were zealous for the worship of Baal. They stood up for their god, when they arose early in the morning, and found that his altar had been thrown down in the night. "Who hath done this thing?" they asked, in hot anger. They demanded the life of Gideon. "Bring out thy son," said they to Joash, "that he may die." Doubtless Gideon had foreseen all this. He knew full well the religious feelings of his fellow-citizens. He knew that his conduct would make him many and powerful enemies. But he had counted the cost; and he knew also whose servant he was, and therefore he rose up in the night, and threw down the altar of Baal, and cut down his grove. If idolaters be zealous for the honour of Baal, he will be no less zealous for the honour and glory of God.

Now, it is just this zeal and this courage, in the face of danger and difficulties, which prove the character of the true Christian. If a man will venture nothing for Christ, he is not worthy of him. Christ will not own him. The world are brave enough for their gods. Look at the votaries of pleasure, and of Mammon, how bold *they* are! Mark the principles and practice of the avowed Sabbath-breakers, hear their bold trumpet-tongued proclamations. They cry aloud, "Down with the Sabbath; what right has the Lord to the whole of the day! Divide it between God and Baal. Away with your sanctimonious bigotry! It is the people's day!" Ah, we need a Gideon to rise up in Israel! Rather, we need, that all the people of God should be as zealous for the true God, for his Word, for his day, for his worship – as idolaters are for the worship of Baal. Be it so, that we be called narrow-minded, unfit to live in this enlightened age, we would rather stand in the latter day, with Gideon and his ten brave servants, than with all the men of the city who pleaded for Baal.

3. Mark, also, that Gideon's obedience *was eminently successful and strikingly rewarded.*

He was for God, and God was for him. The Lord made his way prosperous. Gideon's ten servants did their work well. He was not left to do all the work himself. Doubtless they caught their master's spirit and zeal. It is astonishing how much influence for good or evil, every master exercises over his own household. Eyes are upon him, when he least suspects it.

But Gideon was defended by one who of all others seemed pledged to oppose him. His father was an idolater. It was his father's altar that he threw down, and it was his father's bullock that he offered upon the altar of the Lord. The men of the city full well knew how zealous the old man was for Baal. They fully reckoned upon his devotion to the idol. And, therefore, they came to Joash, and said unto him, "Bring out thy son, that he may die." But the hearts of all men are in the Lord's hand. Joash ceased to be an idolater that very night. Perhaps the bravery of his son – or his steady and consistent piety and zeal, convinced him of his sin; or perhaps the impotency of Baal to save himself, was conclusive logic to his mind. We know not what it was which weighed most with him. Perhaps the whole of the events put together tore the veil from his eyes. Be that as it may, his idolatrous father ceased to be an idolater, and stood up for Gideon and defended his deed. "And Joash said unto all that stood against him, Will ye plead for Baal? Will ye serve him? He that will plead for him, let him be put to death while it is yet morning; if he be a god, let him plead for himself, because one hath cast down his altar."

Who can tell how many fathers and mothers in Israel, how many sons and daughters, relatives and friends, would be converted and saved, were Christian men and women as faithful to their God as was Gideon? You think to conciliate the world by concession, by connivance at their sinful principles and customs. Alas, your inconsistency only leads them to despise you. Be consistent, be uncompromising in serving the Lord; be courageous – obey God rather than man, and God will honour you, as he has honoured many, and made them instruments in winning father and mother, brothers and sisters to Christ. Ah! it would be a terrible thing in the Day of Judgment, for any relative or friend to point his finger at us and say, in the hearing of the assembled world, "Had *you* been as zealous for God, as I was for Baal; had you pleaded as consistently and earnestly for *your* God, as I did for *mine;* had you warned me of the danger of my soul, and proved by your zeal the sincerity of your belief – I should have repented, I should never have been tormented in this flame."

Do not men even now *plead* for Baal? And yet, can he save *himself?* Can he save *you?* Why plead for him longer? I beseech you to be decided for the true God. "Who is on the Lord's side? Who?" Standing before Baal's altar may you say, "Lord, here am I, make me as Gideon. O Lord, come to me. Angel of the covenant, appear to me. Let fire come up out of the rock, and consume the world in my heart. Tell me that Jesus died for me. Tell me that He is my peace. O Holy Spirit, dwell in me, change and sanctify my heart, and assure me that I shall not die. And then, Lord – speak, and thy servant will hear: 'Lord, what wilt thou have me to do?'"

Thus pray, and Baal's altar and Baal's grove will soon fall. The Holy Spirit can and will strengthen you, to cut off the right hand, and pluck out the right eye, and to lay down your very life for Christ. And when this is ready to be done, and God's altar of love is raised in your heart, you will be able to ask in joyful triumph, "What shall we say to these things? If God be for us, who can be against us? Who is he that condemneth? It is Christ that died, yea rather that is risen again, who is even at the right hand of God, who also maketh intercession for us."

5

Nature's Laws

"And Gideon said unto God, If thou wilt save Israel by mine
hand, as thou hast said, behold, I will put a fleece of wool in
the floor; and if the dew be on the fleece only, and it be dry
upon all the earth beside, then shall I know that thou wilt save
Israel by mine hand, as thou hast said. And it was so: for he
rose up early on the morrow, and thrust the fleece together, and
wringed the dew out of the fleece, a bowl full of water.
And Gideon said unto God, Let not thine anger be hot against
me, and I will speak but this once: let me prove, I pray thee,
but this once with the fleece: let it now be dry only upon the
fleece, and upon all the ground let there be dew. And God did
so that night: for it was dry upon the fleece only, and there was
dew on all the ground." (*Judges 6:36-40*)

"Thou from primeval nothingness didst call
First chaos, then existence – Lord, on Thee
Eternity hath its foundation – all
Sprung forth from Thee – of light, joy, harmony.
Sole origin – all life, all beauty Thine.
Thy word created all, and doth create:
Thy splendour fills all space with rays divine.
Thou art, and wert, and shalt be! Glorious! great!
Light-giving, life-sustaining Potentate!"

GIDEON owned the sovereignty, and the power of God. So
must we. In the matter of salvation we deal with Omnipotence.
The God of grace is the Sovereign Ruler of the universe. He reigneth
with absolute sway. None can resist his will. None can withstand his
power. He is God alone.

There is no fickleness in God, no change in his nature. His attributes and perfections are ever the same. He changeth not. Hath He said, and shall He not do it? Hath He spoken, and shall it not stand fast? Change is incidental to the finite. He is infinite in all his glorious perfections. He is, therefore, "the same yesterday, today, and for ever." This is the *sinner's hope:* "I change not, therefore ye sons of Jacob are not consumed." This is *the believer's confidence:* "All the promises in Christ are yea and amen, to the glory of God the Father."

To show his power, to reveal his will, to make manifest his grace and love to the sons of men, he maketh all nature bow to his sceptre. He commandeth the clouds, and they drop fatness. "He causeth it to rain on one city, and causeth it not to rain on another city." He appointeth the sun, and moon, and stars in their courses, and they obey his will. He directeth the flight of the comet, as it speeds from star to star, from system to system. The teeming millions of worlds which immensity contains in her vast bosom, are all doing his behests. Not a star, a planet, a sun, or a system, throughout the mighty sweep of immensity, but doeth his bidding, and fulfilleth his purpose. Not a wave that breaks upon the rocky shore, not a leaf that falls in the untrod forest, not a flower that blooms in the loneliest desert, not a dew-drop which falls in the stillness of the night, but has its mission to perform, in the fulfilment of His counsel who reigneth over all. In the sublime language of the Psalmist, "Fire and hail, snow and vapours, and stormy wind fulfil His word."

Gideon believed in the omnipotence of God. He rested upon his promises. But he wanted a confirmation of his faith in these promises. He seemed to cast his eyes to heaven, and say in language which has often found a response in the hearts of tried believers, "*Show me a token for good;* that they which hate me may see it, and be ashamed; because thou, Lord, hast holpen me, and comforted me." Or, like one struggling to master his doubts and fears, on finding that he could not overcome the natural infidelity of his depraved heart, turned to the stronghold whence alone help could come, and prayed, "Lord, I believe, help thou mine unbelief."

The Lord *did* help his unbelief, by granting him the two-fold miracle for which he prayed. It was a fine instance of childlike confidence in this "mighty man of valour," that as soon as his faith began to waver, he at once told the Lord. Half of our difficulties in the

Christian course would be got over, and got over quickly too, if we would but unbosom our souls to the Lord, and tell Him our difficulties as soon as they arise. We are too apt to keep back from Him the secrets of our hearts – our doubts, our fears, our misgivings. We are more ready to tell a fellow-mortal what doubts becloud our faith, and darken our hopes, than to go, as Gideon did, and tell Him at once that we need some fresh token of His favour and love.

Now, the token vouchsafed to Gideon was peculiar in its nature. He was led, doubtless acting under the influence of the Holy Spirit, to ask of God a sign, and to choose a sign himself. In infinite condescension, God was pleased to accede to his petition. He suspended the ordinary laws of nature, and whether the fleece of wool was to be wet or dry, according to the prayer of this man of God, we are told, "God did so that night."

The grand doctrine to be deduced from this narrative is, *that in confirmation of His promises, and in appearing on behalf of His people, the Lord suspended the ordinary laws of nature.*

Let us elucidate this important point for a few moments.

I. Observe, first, that it was none other than *the Lord Jesus Christ Himself who thus answered Gideon's prayer.*

God, to whom Gideon prayed in *verse 36*, is the same who "looked upon him," and spake to him in *verse 14*. He was the angel of the covenant, who said, "Go in this thy might, and thou shalt save Israel from the hand of the Midianites: have not I sent thee?" Gideon prayed to this same Lord, that He would grant him a sign that He would save Israel by his hand, "as He had said."

The answer to Gideon's prayer – the two-fold miracle which was wrought – proved the proper deity of Christ. It proved that the government of all things was indeed upon his shoulder. His rule and his reign were not limited to the days of his flesh. The mighty and weighty truth embodied in the words of the Apostle, in his Epistle to the Colossians, was as much a matter of fact in the days of Gideon, as it was after the ascension of Christ – "By HIM were all things created, that are in heaven, and that are in earth, visible and invisible, whether they be thrones, or dominions, or principalities, or powers: all things are created BY HIM, and FOR HIM: and he is before all things, and BY HIM all things consist." His dominion is as unlimited as the universe. His absolute power extends not only to his Church, and to man in general, and to devils and angels, but also to all nature – to the whole created universe. All the laws of nature are his laws. He holds the sun in his place. He directs the world in its undeviating orbit. He *only* binds the sweet influences of Pleiades, and He *only* can loose the bands of Orion. He numbers the clouds in wisdom, and stays the bottles of heaven. (*Job 38*). The sunbeam is guided by his eye, and the dew-drops fall at his bidding.

"I am a man under authority," said a Roman centurion to Christ, "and I say to this man, Go, and he goeth: and to another, Come, and he cometh; and to my servant, Do this, and he doeth it." "Speak the word only, and my servant shall be healed." That man trusted in the power of Jesus over disease, and by consequence over nature's laws.

It is in the hands of such a Saviour, that God the Father has placed the salvation of sinners. Rising from the grave, and just re-ascending his glorious throne, he said, "*All* power is given unto me in heaven and in earth." A cold assent to this truth saves no man's soul. We need it as a living principle in the heart. Flesh and blood did not reveal it to Peter: nor was it nature, but grace, which enabled Thomas to exclaim, "My Lord and my God!" "No man can say that Jesus is the Lord, but by the Holy Ghost." To pronounce the words is easy enough. Mechanical effort will avail for that. But to *feel* the truth – to *rest upon* it – to venture into eternity relying upon it – to cling to the Deity of Jesus in the hours of danger and of deaths as the thief clung to it, more closely than the nails fastened him to his cross; to pray as he prayed: "Lord," thou dying, thou bleeding "Lord, remember me when thou comest into thy kingdom;" this is being wise unto salvation – this is accepting the promise of life, this is embracing the deliverance uttered by the Spirit – "Kiss the Son, lest He be angry, and ye perish from the way, when his wrath is kindled but a little. Blessed are all they that put their trust in him." (*Psalm 2:12*).

II. Now, *it is over the laws of nature that Christ reigneth, for the good of his Church in all ages.*

We know not how little, nor how much, other worlds are affected by the redemption of Christ's people in this world. We cannot suppose that the knowledge of the wondrous story of redeeming love is confined to this our tiny planet. It may be that inhabitants of other spheres, and of other systems, are learning the wisdom, and the goodness, and the love of God, in the book of man's salvation.

Angels study it, the highest orders of intelligence make it their theme of praise, and why not beings in untold worlds which fill up the immensity of space? It may be, we say, that yonder worlds look down upon us and watch our doings – our reception or rejection of Him, whose cross was erected on Calvary, and before whose throne they all bow. They might be, for aught we know, joining angels in their songs of praise over one sinner that repenteth; and they might be marvelling at the impenitency of that man who goeth on still in his sins.

But be this as it may, all the laws of the universe are under the rule of the Lord Jesus for the good of His people. There is no law, but the will of God. Nature's laws, as they are called, are naught else but the will of God in uniform operation. Whenever man has discovered this uniformity in nature, he has set it down as a principle, and called it a law of nature. A stone falls to the ground: its tendency is always to do so. This stone obeys, say philosophers, the law of gravitation. We do not object to the term law. It is metaphorical, and it is necessary to use it, perhaps, in the discussion of science and philosophy. But when men talk of universal and eternal laws, whether in morals or science, as if those laws were eternal in themselves, and independent of the one only eternal mind which regulates them all, they talk worse than nonsense – they talk infidelity. There can be no law in operation, in the wide universe, independent of mind and will. To deify law, is to undeify God. So to enthrone nature as to make *her* reign, is to dethrone Jehovah, who *alone* does reign "God over all, blessed for evermore."

Time would fail us to dwell upon the many instances of the suspension of the laws of nature, recorded in the Word of God. We will mention but a few remarkable examples.

1. Observe the suspension of the laws of *physical nature* for the good of the people of God.

Examples spread themselves over the whole Bible. Take the case of the Flood – that fearful deluge which swept all mankind into eternity, with the exception of eight persons. We cannot but observe the merciful object of this awful judgment. "God saw that the wickedness of man was great in the earth, and that every imagination of the thoughts of his heart was only evil continually." What an awful picture of human depravity! How could such a corrupt race live upon the earth, and people the world? History records that whole islands in the South Seas have become wholly depopulated, through the licentiousness, wars, and universal depravity of its inhabitants. Had this earth continued to bear in her bosom, such sons of violence and bloodshed as existed before the flood, there would have been heard, over her waste and barren solitariness, echoed from her bleak rocks, and desolated plains, but one voice, as of old, "Lamentation, and weeping, and great mourning, Rachel weeping for her children, and would not be comforted, because they are not."

No wonder, then, that God arose to judgment, on behalf of his people. "Christ was to see his seed and to be satisfied" – such was the covenant promise, before the foundation of the world. But to human eyes there seemed a likelihood, that that seed would never be born. We read in *Genesis 6:3* – that "the Lord said, My Spirit shall not *always* strive with man." Peter tells us *whose* Spirit *did* strive with these men of violence before the flood. Remarkable is the record in *1 Peter 3:18-20* – "Christ," saith the Apostle, "went by the Spirit, and preached unto them which sometime were disobedient, when once the long-suffering of God waited in the days of Noah, while the ark was a preparing, wherein few, that is, eight souls, were saved by water." Those spirits were in prison when Peter wrote, and were cast into prison at the deluge, and there they will remain until the great Day of Judgment. But the eight souls in the ark were "*saved by water.*" It was water which saved their lives from the violence of the ungodly. It was water which preserved a seed for Christ upon the earth. Men often see nothing but judgment and wrath in the deluge. But they overlook the tenderness, and mercy, and love which watched over the infant race of mankind, and preserved its life amidst the universal destruction going on. God took no pleasure in sweeping the ungodly from the face of the earth. Speaking after the manner of men, in language suited to our comprehension, and expressive of what would have been human feelings, we read that, "It repented the Lord that he had made man on the earth, and it grieved him at his heart." Wrath and destruction are his "strange work." But justice is ever enthroned with love. Truth and mercy are ever living in each other's embrace. It was as much love, as justice, which suspended the laws of nature at the flood. Mercy to Noah and his family was but a type of mercy to all future generations. Faithfulness to the covenant of salvation in Christ Jesus, the everlasting love to all his coming seed, demanded that "Noah should be saved." It was then *love to you*, and *to me*, if we be the true children of Christ, which suspended the laws of nature in the days of the flood, and caused "the fountains of the great deep to be broken up, and the flood gates of heaven to be opened."

From the laws of fluids, we turn to those of *motion*. These, too, have been suspended on behalf of God's people. The motions of all the heavenly bodies are all under the supreme direction of one great mind and will. They observe no law, but that which the Lord impresses upon them. He, who ordains their movements, can change them at his pleasure. To deny this, would be to deny His omnipotence. No less striking was the sign given by the Lord to King Hezekiah, than that which He gave to Gideon – "He brought the shadow ten degrees backward, by which it had gone down in the dial of Ahaz." (*2 Kings 20:11*). How wondrous too was the sign – how palpable the change in nature's laws, in the days of Joshua. "Sun," said that leader of Israel's bands, "Sun, stand thou still upon Gibeon: and thou Moon, in the Valley of Ajalon … So the sun stood still in the midst of heaven, and hasted not to go down about a whole day." (*Joshua 10:12, 13*).

The laws of *gravitation* have also been suspended on behalf of the children of the Lord. Elijah ascended in his body to heaven, and Philip was transported from the desert, on the way to Gaza, and carried by the Spirit through the air to Azotus, upwards of thirty miles distant.

The laws of *chemistry* have been suspended, too, in the preservation of the Lord's saints, "They shall take up serpents: and if they drink any deadly thing it shall not hurt them." Chemical action is directed by the mind and will of our God.

The laws of *heat*, too, have been held in suspense, and made to subserve the will of God in protecting his servants. Three of God's children walked unhurt amidst the burning fiery furnace, the flames of which consumed those who cast them in. If you assume that the elements of the devouring fire were unchanged, and that the change which preserved these men took place in their own persons, and in their clothes, you only multiply the miracle, and add to the number of those laws of nature which were suspended by the will of God.

All these marvellous examples of the Lord's power over his own creatures, go at once to confirm the faith of his people in His never-failing promises. Although heaven and earth should seem to oppose the fulfilment of his Word, although physical impossibilities may raise up a barrier, the top of which no eye of sense can scale, yet the eye of faith soars above all nature, up to nature's God, and rests calmly and peaceably upon his enthroned promise, "When thou passest through *the waters*, I will be with thee: and through the rivers, they shall not overflow thee: when thou walkest through *the fire*, thou shalt not be burned: neither shall the flame kindle upon thee." (*Isaiah 43:2*).

2. We might go on and produce instances of the *like suspension of the laws of animal nature*, in carrying out the purposes of Jehovah on behalf of his people.

Birds of the air, the fish of the sea, and the beasts of the earth, have all obeyed other influences than the laws of their nature, in doing the will of their Creator. The instinct which they possess, is just that law which God sustains in them. Unclean and carnivorous birds forget their own natures, and spread their wings, and, as angels of mercy, visit the prophet in the wilderness, and daily spread his table. The fish devours not Jonah, but, at the word of the Lord, safely lands him on dry ground. The lions, too, become the harmless and friendly companions of Daniel, and not a hair of his head is injured in their den.

But all these instances are surpassed by the change in nature's laws in the animal economy, which took place in a certain man whose history is recorded for our admonition. Pride swelled the heart of Nebuchadnezzar the King of Babylon; his sins and iniquities awakened the rebuke of the prophet Daniel. This king had a vision, and in his vision he saw a watcher and a holy one come down from heaven, who cried aloud, and predicted the judgment which awaited him – "Let his heart be changed from man's, and let a beast's heart be given him; and let seven times pass over him. This matter is by the decree of the watchers, and the demand of the word of the holy ones; to the intent that the living may know that the Most High ruleth in the kingdom of men, and giveth it to whomsoever he will, and setteth up over it the basest of men." And we read that "the thing was fulfilled upon Nebuchadnezzar: and he was driven from men, and did *eat grass as oxen*, and his body was wet with the dew of heaven, till his hairs were grown like eagles' feathers, and his nails like birds' claws." (*Daniel 4:33*). Here was a revulsion of nature's laws! The masticating powers, and digestive organs of a man, assuming the nature of those of an ox! This was a sign then present, and a sign to us in after ages, that the functions of animal nature know no laws, but the mind and will of God. He has appointed them, and He changeth them at his pleasure.

Do we not learn from these examples, from the signs which the Lord has given us, in physical nature, in the animal creation, in the fish of the sea, in the birds of the air, and in man himself, that the Lord holdeth all nature's laws in his hands, and will make them do his bidding for the good of his people? "All things are yours," saith the Apostle to believers, "and ye are Christ's, and Christ is God's." All nature is lying at the foot of his throne, waiting upon Him there to do his will. So that we may say, Not only "fire and hail; snow and vapour; stormy wind, fulfilling his word," but one mind, one will, one rule reigneth, in fulfilment of his promises, over "mountains, and all hills; fruitful trees, and all cedars; beasts and all cattle; creeping things, and flying fowl: kings of the earth, and all people: princes, and all judges of the earth: both young men and maidens: old men, and children." And, oh! that all these would praise the name of the Lord; "for his name alone is excellent: his glory is above the earth and heaven." (*Psalm 148:8-13*).

But what if men seek not his glory? What if pride, like the pride of the King of Babylon, swell the heart? What if men seek not a sign that the Lord is with them, and will save them, as Gideon sought? What if, when God saith, "Ask thee a sign of the Lord thy God: ask it either in the depth, or in the height above," men reply, in the language of the idolatrous and hypocritical king Ahaz, "I will not ask, neither will *I tempt* the Lord." Ah! who can tell how long the Lord will bear with them! Have the watchers ceased to watch? Does no just demand go forth at the word of "the holy ones"? Is there no danger of the heart now hardened in sin becoming changed; not changed indeed into a heart of a new-born child of God, but changed into the heart of a beast, as was changed the heart of the proud king of Babylon? *Sparing grace* now sustains nature's laws. How soon all these might be suspended! The heart which now beats, the blood which now flows, the very life which now exists in this frail body, may soon cease. The slightest change in nature's laws might dash a world from its orbit, and hurl it into oblivion; or wreck a soul in that abyss whose depths have never been sounded. Oh! that, with pious and repentant Hezekiah, the reader may feel the pressure of this weighty subject, and the infinite value of the soul, and breathe forth the prayer, "*What shall be the sign* that the Lord will heal me, and that I shall go up into the house of the Lord?"

We will now concentrate our thoughts, for a few moments, upon the remarkable narrative before us.

You will not fail to observe:

1. Gideon's need of a confirmation of his faith.

The only question with this mighty man of valour was, "Is the Lord indeed with me? Is He on my side? Can I possibly have made any mistake? Will He indeed save Israel by my hand, as He has said? Can I have taken too favourable a view of the vision by night, or of the Lord's appearance to me by day? It is true that I have thrown down the altar of Baal, and cut down his grove; but, instead of any immediate deliverance arising therefrom, the men of the city were about to stone me, and all the Midianites, and the Amalekites, have gathered themselves together. Matters seem to grow worse, rather than better, since the Lord appeared to me under the oak that is in Ophrah! Am I not mistaken? I do not doubt the Lord's *power*. If He *will*, He *can*, save Israel by my hand. But *am I certain* that I have not put too favourable an interpretation upon His wonderful promises? I will ask a sign of the Lord." He did so, and you know with what result.

Reader, are you as anxious as was Gideon, to learn the Lord's will, and to ensure His blessing in your undertakings? Do you make your daily callings a matter of prayer? Do you pause in your worldly business, and inquire with deep anxiety, "Is the Lord with me?" Do you acknowledge Him in all your ways, and thus ensure his promised blessing – that "He shall direct your paths"? Many a man loses his way by seeking no sign from the Lord, that He is with him, to bless and prosper him.

But what if you do prosper in your worldly calling, does no deeper anxiety press upon your mind? Are you quite sure that you will be saved from your enemies? Are you stronger than the Midianites? What if you be left to do battle with eternity alone? What if your sanguine hopes are all futile? What if you are deceived as to the grounds of your salvation? Have you received the sign of the dew from heaven? Can you rest for a moment, without the sealing of the indwelling Spirit, to "bear witness with your spirit, that you are a child of God"? Surely you will not, as a rational being, as a responsible agent, suffer such a momentous question to hang in suspense. As you value your eternal well-being I conjure you, to spread out before the Lord his gracious promises, as Gideon spread the fleece of wool; and rise up early, and go again and again, in faith and prayer, to the throne of grace, and thrust the fleece together, and never cease your importunity, until you wring the dew of the Spirit out of the fleece. The genuineness of your faith will be proved; not by your having no fears, but by the strength of those fears, until you obtain an answer to your prayers. Not once only, but twice, did Gideon prove the Lord; and you too, will prove Him again and again, until all doubts are removed, and you are enabled to say, with Paul, "I know whom I have believed, and am persuaded that He is able to keep that which I have committed unto Him against that day." (*2 Timothy 1:12*).

2. One thought more suggests itself. You see the nature of that proof which the Lord gave to Gideon, that his promises were sure: the dew was given and withheld according to the sign proposed.

We may regard the dew as a striking and beautiful emblem of the Holy Spirit. "I will be as the dew unto Israel," saith the Lord. But He is not as the dew unto any but to *his Israel*. The giving, and withholding of the Spirit is "*the sign*" which the Lord vouchsafes to his people, that He is with them. It is the bedewing of the Spirit which distinguishes the Lord's people from all the rest of mankind. Upon whomsoever that dew descends, pardon through the blood of Jesus descends also, and with that pardon, a more wondrous-working garment than that which fell from the fiery chariot of Elijah.

The dew of the Spirit, so refreshing and welcome to the thirsty soul, seals pardon and peace and salvation. It descends we know not how; but softly, silently, tenderly, upon the broken heart, and contrite spirit. No money can purchase it. The barrenness of no hard rock will hinder its descent. Wheresoever the knee of faith bendeth, there the dew descendeth, according to the promise, "If ye being evil know how to give good gifts unto your children, how much more shall your heavenly Father give the Holy Spirit to them that ask Him?"

6

Pride Dethroned

"And the Lord said unto Gideon, The people that are with thee
are too many for me to give the Midianites into their hands,
lest Israel vaunt themselves against me, saying, *Mine own hand
hath saved me.*" (*Judges 7:2*)

"Deep is the sea, and deep is hell, but pride mineth deeper;
It is coiled as a poisonous worm about the foundations of the soul:
If thou expose it in thy motions, and track it in thy springs of
    thought,
Complacent in its own detection, it will seem indignant virtue;
Smoothly will it gratulate thy skill, O subtle Anatomist of self,
And spurn at its very being, while it nestleth the deeper in thy bosom.
Pride is a double traitor, and betrayeth itself to entrap thee,
Making thee vain of thy self-knowledge; and proud of thy discoveries
    of pride."

PRIDE hurled Satan from heaven, and turned angels into devils.
Pride drove Adam out of Paradise, and barred its gates against
his posterity. Pride of intellect, pride of family, pride of wealth, pride
of power, are adamantine chains, which bind men in fetters of sin.

Boasting and vain-glory, are inherent to fallen nature. Angels,
archangels, and cherubim, who stand in the unveiled presence of
Jehovah, are the most humble of God's creatures, the most conscious
of their own unworthiness.

But fallen man ever boasts of his sufficiency, his goodness, his wisdom, his power. We see this in the look, the language, and the acts of
young children. "Foolishness is bound up in the heart of a child;" so,
too, is pride. Self-will, self-confidence, self-sufficiency, pride – these
are evils which ensnare the child, and follow the man to his grave.

The result of all this is apparent. Man is too proud to be saved by another. He cannot but feel that he needs a Saviour. Conscience, and the Word of God, tell him that he is in danger of future ruin. He does not usually question the fact. But his pride questions the *plan of deliverance*. He is aware that he has "fallen," and greatly fallen too, "by his iniquity." But he is not prepared to believe, that in the Lord *alone*, is his help. Pride says he can help himself – if not much – yet a little. He does not, if he reads the Bible, deny that he cannot be saved without grace. Protestant or Romanist, he consents to his need of grace. But pride whispers in his heart, that if grace help him, he also can help grace. He will not believe that he can do nothing, and that God must do everything.

Now, pride is a blind sin. It is an illogical sin. It has lost all sound logic in theology. I very much question whether proud intelligences in hell understand true divinity. I am sure no proud *man* does. He does not see the consequences of his own creed, the result of his own hopes.

Let man help grace to save him, and what would be the result? Why, just in proportion that man helped God, he would "vaunt himself" against God. He would swell with pride. He would claim a share of God's glory!

Now, God will not give his glory to another. He is a jealous God – jealous of his own honour, majesty, glory. He must be so, or be no God. How then is man's pride, and boasting, to be kept down, and at length stamped out? The Apostle Paul asked this same question of the Roman Christians: "Where is boasting then? It is excluded. By what law?" By what rule? By what plan of salvation? "Of works?" "Of works," in whole or in part? "Nay." "Works" make room for boasting. *They* would put great swelling words into man's mouth, and make him say, "I thank God that I am not as other men are." "Nay, but by the law of faith." "Therefore we conclude that a man is justified by faith, without the deeds of the law." (*Romans 3:27, 28*).

The history of Gideon illustrates these points. The Israelites were oppressed by their enemies. They made an effort to shake off their chains of bondage. But the Midianites and their confederates, the Amalekites, and all the children of the East, like grasshoppers for multitude; and their camels without number, as the sand by the sea-side for multitude; altogether at least 150,000 men, came up against

Israel. The Lord raised up Gideon to destroy these enemies of his people. This brave man gathered together a small, and probably an undisciplined army, amounting to 32,000 men. A small and unequal band to oppose 150,000! If this small army conquer the hosts of Midian, they will boast that it was their sword which gave them the victory. The Lord therefore, determines so to reduce their numbers, that His hand *alone*, may be seen in the discomfiture of their enemies. He reduces the 32,000 to 10,000, and then the 10,000 to 300! And the Lord said, "By the 300 will I deliver the Midianites into thine hand."

Thus 300 were to gain the victory over 150,000! Comparison of strength there could be none! It would be ridiculous to talk of means suited to the end now! There was no human might, no human power left! If the victory be on the side of Israel, every tongue must confess, that "it is the Lord's doing." This was just what God intended. He meant to humble man, and exalt Himself. Man's pride was to be laid low in the dust. Gideon, when he looked at his 32,000 men, doubtless thought *they* were *too few;* but God said to him, "The people that are with thee are *too many* for me to give the Midianites into their hands, lest Israel vaunt themselves against me, saying, Mine own hand hath saved me."

Now, there are three things to be noticed here: 1. *The Lord's jealousy of his own glory.* 2. *Man's tendency to "vaunt himself" against the Lord.* 3. *Man humbled, and the Lord exalted.*

The Lord's Jealousy of His Own Glory

We have a *remarkable instance of the Lord's jealousy of his own honour and glory.* The Lord made all things, and sustains all things, in heaven and in earth, for his own glory. No end or object short of this, would be worthy of Himself. The happiness of all creatures, is bound up in the honour of the Creator. God seeks therefore, the good of all, when He seeks his own glory. The ruin of all, would follow the dethronement of Himself. Redeemed spirits in heaven own this. (*Revelation 4:10, 11*).

Salvation is *essentially* for the happiness of God's people. But it is supremely for the glory of God. The two objects are inseparably united in the one end. Let us look at this in the case of Gideon.

The Lord *gives* the victory to Israel *as a free gift.* The great danger in employing Israel at all in the battle, was, lest they should say, "Mine own hand hath saved me." But the reduction of their numbers to 300, was sufficient to show them, that it was not *their* hand that saved them, but the Lord's sovereign mercy.

Now, the salvation of the sinner is just as much a *free gift*, as was Gideon's victory. There is no more fitness in the creature to win heaven, than there was power in these 300 to win the victory. We are as powerless to help ourselves, as were they. "This is the word of the Lord unto Zerubbabel, saying, Not by might, not by power, but by my Spirit, saith the Lord of hosts." And why is this? Surely, that "no flesh should glory in the Lord's presence!" Lest Israel vaunt themselves, and say, "Mine own hand hath saved me."

How full is the Word of God respecting the freeness of salvation! Both examples and declarations abound. Was Abraham saved by his own hand? Did his obedience save him? Did the wisdom of Daniel save him? Was David saved by his own virtue? Did Manasseh's good works save him? What saved Mary Magdalene, but the sovereign grace of God? What but the Lord's mercy, plucked Paul, as a brand from the burning, on his way to Damascus? What part had the backsliding, Christ-denying Peter, in his own salvation? What might was there in the hand of the thief on the cross, to save his own soul? Go through the whole Bible, and you will not find a single instance recorded of any man, being able to "vaunt himself against the Lord," and say, "My own hand hath saved me."

Examine for a moment the plain and reiterated declarations in Scripture, to the same effect. Where shall we begin? Shall we speak of our *calling?* It is God's gift. "It pleased God who called me by his grace," said Paul. (*Galatians 1:15*). Shall we look at our *adoption?* It is God's gift. We are adopted "according to the good pleasure of his will." (*Ephesians 1:5*). Shall we examine our *regeneration?* It is the gift of God. "We are born not of blood, nor of the will of the flesh, nor of the will of man, but of God." (*John 1:13*). Shall we turn to our *justification?* That also is the gift of God. "Being justified freely by his grace." (*Romans 3:24*). Is *faith* essential to salvation? That is the gift of God. "They believed through grace." (*Acts 18:27*). Is *repentance* looked at? That, too, is the gift of God. "If God will peradventure give them repentance." (*2 Timothy 2:25*). Is *sanctification* essential? That, too, is God's gift. "The very God of peace sanctify you wholly." (*1 Thessalonians 5:23*). Is *perseverance* unto the end considered? That, too, is the free gift of God. "Who shall also confirm you unto the end." (*1 Corinthians 1:8*). Will you go one step further, and ask whence is salvation and eternal life? That, too, is God's own free gift. "By grace are ye saved through faith; and that not of yourselves: it is the gift of God." (*Ephesians 2:8*). What need we more? This absolute freeness of grace and glory, this gift of victory over sin, death, and hell, and this final triumph through the arm of the Lord, are revealed so fully, so repeatedly, that all the glory of salvation, from first to last, may be ascribed to the Lord alone. The Lord *thus* saves, and *thus* glorifies the sinner, "that no flesh should glory in His presence." (*1 Corinthians 1:29*). But that, "according as it is written, He that glorieth, let him glory in the Lord." (*1 Corinthians 1:31*).

How wise, then, and how pious was the prayer of Asaph: "Help us, O God of our salvation, for the glory of thy name." (*Psalm 79:9*). And how touchingly beautiful, and scriptural, are the two responses in our Church Litany! In the first we pray, "Lord, arise, help us, and deliver us, *for thy Name's sake*." And then, deepening in intensity of petition, and rising to the highest plea of entreaty, we cry, "O Lord, arise, help us, and deliver us, *for thine honour*." We cannot go beyond this. Here God himself stops. Salvation, from first to last, is, "according to the good pleasure of his will, to the praise of the glory of his grace." (*Ephesians 1:5, 6*). He will not admit, therefore, any intermixture of human merit, deserts, or might. He will humble man in the very dust, lest he should vaunt himself against Him, and say, "Mine own hand hath saved me."

Man's Tendency to Vaunt Himself

Now mark man's tendency to vaunt himself against the Lord.

We may truly say of every man what Joash said to Amaziah, "Thine heart lifteth thee up to boast." The Apostle draws up a black catalogue of those who did not like to retain God in their knowledge; and amongst them he enumerates "whisperers, backbiters, haters of God, despiteful, *proud, boasters*." The same Apostle warned his son Timothy against the same characters: "In the last days perilous times shall come. For men shall be lovers of their own selves, covetous, *boasters, proud*, blasphemers."

Vainglory is natural to the human heart. In the fable of the ancients, the fly that sat on the axletree of the chariot-wheel, gave out that she made the glorious dust of the chariot. God rebukes the same pride in forcible language – "I will punish," He saith, "the fruit of the stout heart of the king of Assyria, and the glory of his high looks." And then He asketh, respecting him, and respecting all such vain-glorious men – "Shall the axe boast itself against him that heweth therewith? or shall the saw magnify itself against him that shaketh it?" Let Israel's bands, by their own sword, overcome the Midianites, and they will at once "vaunt themselves against the Lord, and say, Mine own hand hath saved me."

Sin is proud. It is a vaunting, a boasting evil, against God. It exalts itself at the expense of God's glory. It dwelt in the heart of Satan, and would rather reign in hell, than serve in heaven. It entered paradise, and said to Adam and Eve, "Ye shall be as gods." It would ever be making gods of men, at the expense of undeifying God Himself. No sin begins sooner in the heart, and no sin leaves us later, than this pride. It is like the heart itself, the first thing that lives, and the last thing that dies in us.

When, therefore, the Lord visits the sinner with grace, grace is at once opposed by pride, "I will save thee," saith the Lord. "Be it so," saith the sinner. But "I will save thee *freely*," saith the Lord. "Freely?" saith the sinner. "But what am *I* to do? Am I to do nothing? Are my good works to go for nothing? God! I thank thee that I am not so bad as some other men are!" Thus pride speaks, and would vaunt itself against the Lord, and say, "Mine own hand hath saved me, or at least *helped* to save me."

Do any doubt this? Think you that we are drawing colours too deep. Look for a moment:

1. *At man's notion respecting some good thing still remaining in his heart, notwithstanding his fall.* How few really believe in the *total depravity* of the natural heart! Popery and Arminianism say, "Man has power left to turn to God, if he will. Let him only put forth nature's strength, and grace will help him."

Our Church, on the contrary, teaches her children that "they have no power to do good works pleasant and acceptable to God, without the grace of God in Christ *preventing* them, that they may have a good will." It teaches them, moreover, that original sin, "in every person born into this world, deserveth God's wrath and damnation." The Word of God is equally strong. The Apostle Paul saith, "We were by nature children of wrath, even as others." And, speaking of himself, he saith, "In me," that is, in my flesh, "there dwelleth no good thing."

Now, pride vaunts itself against the Lord, and will not admit of this truth. Pride rebels against the plan God has laid down for man's salvation – "By grace are ye saved through faith; and that not of your-selves; it is the gift of God; not of works, lest any man should *boast*." The natural heart is set upon boasting, and therefore proudly rejects this humiliating doctrine. Give pride but one inch of creature good in the human heart, and it has a fulcrum for its lever, which would move the crown from the head of the Son of God. It would vaunt itself against the Lord, and say, "Mine own hand hath saved me."

2. Again look at *man's notion respecting the only ground of the sinner's acceptance before God*. The vaunting of the first-named evil, is against God the Holy Ghost: boasting that *He* need not do everything *in* the soul. This vaunting is against God the Son, boasting, that *He* need not do everything *for* the soul. Sanctification and Justification are cardinal points in the Christian's creed. Pride vaunts itself against both; and denies the scriptural nature of both. There were certain people in the apostle's day, who "being ignorant of God's righteous-ness," that is, of God's plan of justifying the sinner in the obedience of Christ, "and going about to establish their own righteousness, did not submit themselves unto the righteousness of God." Pride would not suffer them to stoop to this humiliating plan of being reckoned just before God. They believed that there was some good in them-selves, by which they could do good, and thus effect something, more or less, towards their own justification.

Now men reject, with pride, the humiliating doctrine that as "Christ *died* for the ungodly," so "God *justifieth* the ungodly," as the Apostle Paul teaches us. They would cease being accounted "ungodly," *before* they believe that God can justify them. They do not under-stand practically, and pride rejects the truths that Christ came, "*not* to call the *righteous*, but *sinners* to repentance." Pride craves a footing for self-righteousness. Let *Christ* do all *He* can, and let the *sinner* do all *he* can, and then God will be justified in justifying him. Nay, saith God, justification must be all of works, or all of grace. There can be no union of the two. Christ *or* man, not Christ *and* man, are the terms laid down in the Scriptures. The sinner whose hope in him-self is all gone, and gone for ever, thankfully, and joyfully, embraces this plan of salvation. He casts himself into the arms of Christ, and saith – "Be *thou alone* my righteousness." But proud human nature vaunteth itself against the Lord, and saith, "Mine own hand will *help* to save me."

Man Humbled and the Lord Exalted

The third point illustrated by the narrative before us, is the means by which the Lord humbled man, and exalted Himself.

The Lord is at no loss for means to carry out his purpose. All means are at his disposal. He knows full well *how* to bring down the proud looks of men.

The means employed in the present case were two-fold:

1. *He reduced Gideon's army* of 32,000, by 22,000, who were "fearful and afraid" – timid – in other words – *cowards*. All these he commanded to go to their homes. Their own fears and consciences told them that they were cowards, and unfit for war, and therefore, they should not remain to boast that they won the victory.

2. Then the Lord *further reduced* the remaining 10,000 by 9,700, whom He knew would vaunt themselves against himself, and say, "*We* won the victory." Three hundred only were left! These were the flower of the army. All true men. They could be relied upon in the day of trial. "By the 300," saith the Lord, "will I save you." Thus Gideon's army was reduced. Doubtless his faith was greatly tried. But all "boasting was excluded." If Israel be saved, it will be worse than folly to talk of their own power saving them. Anything short of this reduction might have left room for *some* vainglory. But 300 against 150,000, what could *they* do! Thus the Lord brought down the power and the pride of Israel, lest they should vaunt themselves against Him, and say, "Mine own hand hath saved me."

Now, there is a counterpart to all this in grace. The Lord will bring down the pride of a man, if He save him. He will secure to himself all the glory of the sinner's salvation. "The mean man shall be brought down, and the mighty man shall be humbled, and the eyes of the lofty shall be humbled: and the Lord of hosts shall be exalted in judgment, and God, that is holy, shall be sanctified in righteousness." So spake the Spirit in Isaiah. The language of Paul is similar: "Ye see your calling, brethren, how that not many wise men after the flesh, not many mighty, not many noble, are called; but God hath chosen the foolish things of the world, to confound the wise: and God hath chosen the weak things of the world, to confound the things that are mighty: and base things of the world, and things which are despised, hath God chosen, yea, and things which are not, to bring to nought things that are; that no flesh should glory in his presence."

Look at Gideon's 22,000 brave men! They do not face the enemy. They turn back before they draw a sword. In the dead of the night they all skulk away. Ah! how many brave talkers are there in every age, in every Church! Loud boasters, but cowardly doers! Summer Christians! Fair weather sailors! True children of Lot's wife! Quickly they put their hand to the plough, and as quickly look back. Ah! how would they boast, and vaunt themselves against the Lord, if they were saved in their present state! They would walk proudly about the golden street of the heavenly Jerusalem, and none would be so worthy as they, to tread its crystal pavement! Ah! let them return – let them go home! They are unfit for the kingdom of heaven. God will not give victory to them, nor trust his honour in their safe keeping. Israel shall be saved, but not by their sword. God will be glorified, but not by their vainglory.

But the remainder of Gideon's army is more promising. There are still 10,000 with him, standing around his standard at morning light. They look brave! They stand well to arms! Their nerves are strong! They have no doubt themselves of their courage! But "God is greater than their hearts, and knoweth all things." We are not told, but possibly they, too, would have turned back in the day of battle. But be that as it may, only 300 of their number were chosen. These were picked men. Men ready to jeopardise their lives at the word of the Lord. Men of faith. Men who trusted not in sword, or spear, or battle-axe, but only in the word of the Lord. They were brave souls. One of them could turn to flight an army of aliens. One of them could, and did, chase a thousand. These are the men we need in the Church. Men of faith, men of prayer!

Thank God, many of such are spread over favoured England, and over the world. But where are the brave, humble, God-believing, God-honouring men among ourselves? Men of resolute, firm, determined purpose! No boasters! No vaunters! Not self-willed! Not proud! But men of faith, who feel their weakness, and yet their power! Men ready ever to ascribe all victory, all success, all glory to

God, and to say, "Not unto us, O Lord, not unto us, but unto thy name give glory."

We learn, then, from the whole subject:

1. That reduction of external means may be God's way of giving success.

Man's extremity is God's opportunity. The Lord is so jealous of His honour and glory in the Church, that He will "overturn, overturn, overturn, until he come whose right it is: and he will give it him." Be not discouraged, then, if God cut down numerical strength. What if 32,000 be reduced to 300? "If God be for us, who can be against us?" "What are all the hosts of Midian to the Lord!" He can make them turn their swords against each other. What if some vaunting Sennacherib boast himself against Zion? The Lord knows all about it. "I know thine abode, and thy going out, and thy coming in, and thy rage against me." He regards the wicked man's rage against his people, as rage against Himself. "Because thy rage against me, and thy tumult is come up into mine ears, therefore will I put my hook in thy nose, and my bridle in thy lips, and I will turn thee back by the way by which thou camest." You see the Lord will do all this – do it all himself. Israel shall "stand still, and see the salvation of the Lord." The help that is done upon earth, he doeth it himself. Thus boasting is excluded, whilst the victory is ensured. His people have the victory, but God has the glory. And none can vaunt themselves against Him, and say, "Mine own hand hath saved me."

2. Mark also, that the Lord thus manifests his tender care for his own people.

The ungodly, like the Midianites, count the people of God "as sheep for the slaughter." They think they can swallow them up as in a moment. They treat them with scorn and contempt, and as "the offscouring of all things." They boast like proud Goliath against the stripling David, and say, "Come, and we will give your flesh to the fowls of the air." But they forget that the Lord regards the cause of his people as his own. They forget that He hath said, "He that toucheth you, toucheth the apple of mine eye." Oh! how sensitive is God to all injuries done wrongfully to the least of his saints! "Whoso shall offend one of these little ones which believe in me, it were better for him that a millstone were hanged about his neck, and that he were drowned in the depths of the sea." Christ was hated, persecuted, down-trodden, falsely-accused, murdered! But what became of his persecutors and murderers? Where are they now? Ah! God utters a terrible warning to the ungodly, when He saith, "Touch not mine anointed, and do my prophets no harm."

But what if they do rise up and take counsel against the Lord, and against his holy child Jesus? Can they prevail? "Heaven and earth," saith the Lord, "shall pass away, but my word shall not pass away." "Fear not, then, little flock, it is your Father's good pleasure to give you the kingdom." The storms and the tempests at sea, will make the haven more precious. The sharpness of the conflict upon earth, will make heaven more sweet. The louder the clang of arms *here*, the louder far the shout of victory *there*. And when *there*, we will not vaunt ourselves against the Lord, as though our own arm had saved us, but we will hasten to join with those who sing with a loud voice, saying, "Worthy is the Lamb that was slain to receive power, and riches, and wisdom, and strength, and honour, and glory, and blessing."

7

The Trumpet's Blast

"The three companies blew the trumpets, and brake the
pitchers." (*Judges 7:20*)

"Soldier, rest – but not for thee
   Spreads the world her downy pillow:
On the rock thy couch must be,
   While around thee chafes the billow:
Thine must be a watchful sleep,
   Wearier than another's waking;
Such a charge as thou dost keep
   Brooks no moment of forsaking,
     Sleep, as on the battlefield,
     Girded – grasping sword and shield:
Those thou canst not name or number,
Steal upon thy broken slumber."

WE now enter the battlefield. The real conflict is now about to
commence. Hitherto we have been watching the prepara-
tions. The elements of war have been gathering. Now they are about
to burst. We cannot doubt the result. Although Gideon's arm was
weak, his faith was strong. The Midianites might well laugh to scorn
his sword, and *his* feeble band of three hundred. But what power could
withstand – what host will not yield to the blow of that weapon now
drawn from its scabbard, "The sword of the Lord, and of Gideon"?

Gideon had been well trained. This was not his first battle. Before
the angel's visit under the oak which was in Ophrah, he was "a mighty
man of valour." But now the true source of his might was put to the
test: and severely too. It was his faith which made him strong, and
obedient too. It was his faith which cast down Baal's altar, and cut

down Baal's grove. It was faith which blew his trumpet, and gathered together the army of 32,000.

The Lord tried this faith, before He crowned it. The reduction of his followers from 32,000 to 10,000, and then again to 300, was a crucible which melted faith down, and took away the dross. The pure gold now shone brightly.

The people of God often forget *for what* they pray, when they ask for great faith, burning love, ardent zeal, and stern obedience. The Lord never wastes his gifts. There is no waste in nature. There is no waste in grace. The good seed is sown to bear good fruit. If these graces of the Spirit be sown in the heart, God will make their fruits to spring forth. They are sown for the sake of their fruit. Summer and winter, storm and tempest, heat and frost, must all pass over them to bring them to perfection. Great grace is given and implanted in the soul, not to lie dormant there, but to spring up in due season, and bear fruit to the glory of God, in spite of great difficulties, great trials, great temptations, great adversaries.

Opportunities, it is said, make great men. True. But no opportunities make little men great. Little men prove their littleness in emergencies. Great men prove their greatness in the midst of difficulties. The strength of the oak is proclaimed by the might of the storm and the tempest, which uproots a forest of saplings. "If thou faint in the day of adversity, thy strength is small." (*Proverbs 24:10*).

Now Gideon did not faint. He waxed, like David when opposed to Saul, stronger and stronger. His strength was unseen, but it was not unfelt. His enemies dreaded his name, and quailed before his sword. But it was not his own sword which was to save him, and Israel. It was not his own military skill which was to settle the order of battle. His strength was the Lord's promise. His victory would be gained, not by his own sword, but by "the sword of the Lord, and of Gideon."

Let us approach the scene of action. Three objects at once attract our attention, and awaken our interest: 1. *The Companies Engaged*, 2. *The Trumpet's Blast*, 3. *The Pitchers Broken*.

The Companies Engaged

Gideon's 300 men were divided by him into three companies of 100 men each. He placed himself at the head of one of these companies. He instructed his whole army to do as he would do. It was the Lord who chose these 300 brave men, by whom he promised to save Israel. How honoured were they! How distinguished from their fellow-countrymen. It was the Lord who made them to differ. We cannot doubt but that Gideon's faith was theirs. It required on their part great faith to obey Gideon's voice, to stand as they stood, and to act as they acted, in the face of 150,000 armed men. Doubtless the 22,000 faint-hearted men who had gone to their homes, applauded their zeal, their courage, and their faith, after the battle was over, and the victory had been won.

But these three hundred dared to be singular. God called them; Gideon had need of them; their country's safety depended upon them; and they took their lives in their hands, and bravely did battle with the enemy.

Perhaps, too, the 9,700 did not repine at their release from active service. The odds seemed to be against Gideon. At all events, they had no great faith in his divine mission. They looked to an arm of flesh, and had they shared the victory, they would have claimed it for their own, and "vaunted themselves against the Lord, and said, Mine own arm hath saved me."

Now all Christians are baptised to be good soldiers of Jesus Christ. We have all enlisted under the banner of the cross, and sworn "not to be ashamed to confess the faith of Christ crucified, and manfully to fight under his banner against sin, the world, and the devil; and to continue Christ's faithful soldiers and servants unto our life's end." But, alas! when the day of trial comes – when the enemy musters his hosts, when the banners of the world, the flesh, and the devil float in the breeze and far more appear *against* us, than those who are *with* us – how many faint-hearted soldiers appear – how many rush to their homes, and hide themselves for very fear? – how many congratulate themselves that others do battle, whilst they look on, and hope to reap the fruits of victory?

But men are mistaken. The enemy has deceived them. The battlefield is every man's *own* heart. He cannot retire from *that*. He must stand to arms; he must conquer, or perish. There is no middle course. He cannot stand idly by, look on, and clap his hands at victories won by others, and be safe. If he turn back in the day of battle, we know his end. "If any man draw back, my soul shall have no pleasure in him."

Happy, then, is he who is numbered among the three hundred. Be it so that he is in the minority. Many have forsaken him; more are against him. But he is invincible for all that, as long as he does battle with but one weapon, "The sword of the Lord, and of Gideon."

The Trumpet's Blast

Never did means appear more contemptible than those employed by Gideon. Putting aside numerical strength, – 300 against 150,000, – what are we to say of the instruments of war – trumpets, and pitchers, and lamps! How childish! Surely Gideon must be in his dotage! "Am I a dog, that thou comest to me with staves? And the Philistine cursed David by his gods."

Thus the Lord teaches us that means are weak, or strong, just according to His appointment. Weak means are strong, powerful, and all-prevailing, when He ordains the end to be fulfilled by them. When God blesses, the worm Jacob can lift up his head, and thresh the mountains.

But the mightiest instruments are nothing without his blessing. "The strong shall be as tow, and the maker of it as a spark, and they shall both burn together, and none shall quench them." What were 150,000 Midianites when opposed to the blessing of God? What was the army of 185,000 which Sennacherib posted against Jerusalem, when the Lord said, "I will defend this city to save it"? What was the invincible Spanish Armada, when arrayed against his protecting providence, who "held the winds in his fists"?

What was giant Goliath's towering height and sinewy arm, when opposed to David's prayer, David's pebble from the brook, and David's God? Let ungodly sinners learn, that when opposed to God and his people, man's wisdom is folly, man's power is weakness, and man's boasting is madness. "Surely men of low degree are vanity, and men of high degree are a lie: to be laid in the balance, they are altogether lighter than vanity. Trust not in oppression, become not vain in robbery: if riches increase, set not your heart upon them. God hath spoken once; twice have I heard this, that power belongeth unto God."

Now, we have here, in the trumpet's blast, the pitchers broken, and the lamps held forth, striking and appropriate emblems of the preaching of the Gospel. They are fit emblems of the weakness of the instrument, and of the power of its effects.

The preaching of the everlasting Gospel is as the blowing of Gideon's trumpets. What less likely to beat down the strongholds of Satan, than the sweet notes which swell from the silver trumpets of the Gospel? How apparently inadequate the means to the end! How weak, how foolish! Men must be fanatics to suppose that men's evil passions will be subdued, that the love of sin will be uprooted, that their affections will ever be turned heavenward, by preaching nothing but Jesus Christ and Him crucified. Human nature, says the world, needs something different.

If you wish to convert the heathen, civilise them first, and then preach the Gospel to them. If you would reclaim the ungodly among ourselves, do not shock their prejudices. Adapt your preaching to their tastes, their habits, their associations. If you must blow the trumpet, do not alarm them in their sleep, do not startle them. Give them time to awaken, to look about them, to prepare themselves for the reception of truth. Blow the trumpet softly; please their ears; gratify their tastes; play upon their imaginations; awaken dormant feelings. Show them the unreasonableness of sin, the beauty of holiness, and the attractiveness of a virtuous life. Thus preach the Gospel – thus blow the trumpet, and all men will be gratified – and "all men will speak well of you."

In these ways men, "not knowing the Scriptures, nor the power of God," would have the trumpet blown. What would follow, were their advice followed? Paul asks a solemn question, "If the trumpet give an uncertain sound, who shall prepare himself to the battle?" And the Lord himself saith, "If the watchmen see the sword come, and blow not the trumpet, and the people be not warned; if the sword come, and take any person from among them, he is taken away in his iniquity; but his blood will I require at the watchman's hand."

We dare not, then, listen to the suggestion, "Preach smooth things." Our *own souls* are cast into the scales.

But we ask, whence is this, that man ventures to dictate to God? Whence this presumption of the creature, who turns round upon his Maker, and saith, "Thy trumpet must not sound so loud in mine ears – thou dost not know my heart – thou must win me to thyself by other means"? Alas! men know not that the "carnal mind is enmity against God," and therefore enmity against the certain, clear, distinct sounds of the Gospel trumpet. When thus they oppose the preaching of the Gospel, they forget the words of the Lord Jesus, "The truth shall make you free."

But let us turn from man to God. He who made the trumpet, knew full well its power. He would not put the trumpet into our hands, and bid us blow, if the breath of his power were not ready to go forth with the blast.

What saith the Lord? This is the grand question. Paul put the Gospel trumpet to his lips, and sounded forth its notes in Corinth, in Athens, in Ephesus, in Philippi. Did no effects follow? He was oppressed, he was persecuted, he was hated, he was imprisoned, he was stoned. But did man's rage, and Satan's fury destroy the power of the trumpet? "The preaching of the cross," he said, "is to them that perish foolishness; but unto us who are saved, it is the power of God." Did he soften down the tones of the trumpet, to suit the ears of men? Did he flatter the polished Athenian, did he preach philosophy to the learned Corinthian? "My speech and my preaching," he declares, "was not with enticing words of man's wisdom, but in demonstration of the Spirit and of power: that your faith should not stand in the wisdom of men, but in the power of God." Did he withhold unsavoury truths? Did he lower the standard of the cross to suit the preconceived opinions, the prejudices, the tastes, the character of his hearers? Surely he tells us he was "all things to all men," that he "pleased all men in all things," and sought to "give none offence." Did he, therefore, compromise the truth? Was Paul a disciple of expediency? Did he seek to win souls to Christ and heaven, by blowing other than the Gospel trumpet, or by inventing a method by which its loud and clear notes might harmonise with the cadence of man's sins? Nay, standing on the Rock of Ages, and raising the silver trumpet to his lips, he sounded forth in the ears of the elders of the Church of Ephesus, "Wherefore I take you to record this day, that I am pure from the blood of all men. For I have not shunned to declare unto you *all the counsel of God.*" (*Acts 20:26, 27*).

We know the results of such trumpet blasts. No human, no satanic power, could stand against them. The walls of Jericho fell down flat before the sound of the trumpets of rams' horns, and the shout of the people. Higher and still stronger walls than those which surrounded Jericho have fallen, before the clear notes of the Gospel. The powers of darkness quail before this trumpet. The dead in trespasses and sins hear the voice of the Son of God, and they that hear do live, and live for ever. Whilst uncertain sounds, a Gospel which is not the Gospel, settle men in their sins, and cause sport to devils, the clear blast of this trumpet shakes the infernal kingdom to its centre, spreads jubilee among the slaves of earth, and awakens joy in the presence of the angels. Ah! could we but follow the example of the brave and God-trusting 300, and encompass the enemy's camp, and blow the trumpet; could we but engirdle the whole earth with the sweet notes of the everlasting Gospel, confusion, dismay, terror, and destruction would reign amongst the hosts of Christ's enemies – Israel would be saved, and God would be glorified.

We pause to ask you, dear reader, have these gladsome notes sounded in your ears in the dead night of your soul? Have you been awakened by the loud blasts of the Gospel trumpet? Has this trumpet aroused you? Has it called you to a sense of your danger? Has it startled you in your sins? Has it destroyed fatal slumberings? Has it broken your midnight sleep? Has it set you against yourself? Has it caused you to spring up on your feet, draw your sword, and slay your companions – your inbred sins and corruptions? In short, has the trumpet put you to flight? Has it led you to flee into the arms of Jesus, from the wrath to come? If it has not done this, we know of no other trumpet to arouse you. If the silver trumpet fail to awaken you, "you would not be persuaded though one rose from the dead."

But oh! I would ask you, "How shall you escape, if you neglect so great salvation?" What hope remains, if God's voice in his Gospel does not awaken you? Are you prepared to resist every call? Is your heart stout enough to brave every blast of the trumpet? What if you despise those who blow? What if those who hold earthen pitchers in their hands, be men of like passions with yourself – will you turn a deaf ear to the music of the Gospel which swells from their lips? It may appear a small thing to despise or neglect the trumpet *now*. But what will become of those who learn for the first time to obey its summons, when "the Lord himself shall descend from heaven with a shout, with the voice of the Archangel, and with the trump of God"?

The Pitchers Broken

Earthen pitchers seemed to be of all things the most absurd to fight with. The three companies might do some execution were they fully equipped. Trumpets might alarm and terrify, but what could *pitchers* do? How astonished must have been these 300 men, when Gideon said, "Arm yourselves with pitchers"!

The result proved the efficiency of these contemptible instruments. *They* did what no sword, no battle-axe, no spear could do. They held the light, they contained the lamps. They were nothing in themselves, but they were everything to the enterprise. They were powerless in themselves – they were brought into the battlefield for the purpose of being broken to pieces. They were to convey the lights, and then their work was done. Had there been no pitchers in Gideon's army, the means of victory had been wanting. Had the pitchers not been broken, the lamps within them would have been useless.

Now, we have in these pitchers, a striking emblem of the ministers of the Gospel. They are earthen vessels, carrying the lamp of life. They are nothing in themselves. They have no power to turn to flight the armies of the aliens. They have no might to contend against the powers of darkness. But they are charged with light. They hold the lamp of life. It is for this that they are made ministers. It is for the sake of the lamp that they are carried into the battlefield. If the light which is in them be darkness, how great is that darkness. "The blind then lead the blind, and both fall into the ditch," and both fall into the hands of the enemy. Dark pitchers hinder the way of the victors. They darken the path of warriors. They stand in the way of the salvation of souls. They ruin the cause they undertake to serve. Far better that they had never been born, than be as pitchers without lamps.

But faithful ministers contain light, and give light. They guide others to victory. They are vessels made to honour, and their honour is, that next to being saved themselves, they lighten others to glory. Jesus is a "light to lighten the Gentiles;" and He, by the Spirit, has sent his ministers forth, charged with his light. They have no light in themselves. They need as much light from Him, as do others. They are opaque. They were once, even as others, in total darkness, children of wrath. The lamp that they hold is lit by Christ, and is fed by the oil of the Holy Spirit. Once let the oil cease to flow, and they become as other men – aye, and far worse than any. But with this light, and this oil, the meanest pitcher contains more pure light to guide the soul to victory, than the sun in his meridian brightness. Paul felt this, and taught this. He impressed these solemn truths upon the minds of the Corinthian Christians. We would desire to fasten his words upon our own minds and consciences. "We preach not ourselves," said the Apostle, "but Christ Jesus the Lord; and ourselves your servants for Jesus' sake. For God, who commanded the light to shine out of darkness, hath shined in our hearts to give the light of the knowledge of the glory of God in the face of Jesus Christ. But we have this treasure," that is, this light – the light of the knowledge of the glory of God in the face of Jesus Christ, "*in earthen vessels*, that the excellency of the power may be of God, and not of us."

The power of the light then, is in the "earthen vessel." Its excellency is there. There, too, is the knowledge of God in Christ. There it shines, as once shone light out of darkness at the creation of the world. And *how* does it shine forth? "We preach not ourselves, but Christ Jesus the Lord." For *what purpose* does it shine? To give light *to you* whose servants we are, for Jesus' sake.

We see then, the use of these earthen pitchers in the day of battle. They are nothing in themselves: they are made to be broken, to be cast aside when their work is done. But they contain the lamp – that lamp is knowledge – that lamp is the excellency of God's power.

We ask then – and does not the value of your never-dying interests compel us to ask you? – have *you* seen this light? have *you* been guided by that lamp? Has it shone into *your* mind, and given *you* the saving knowledge of the glory of God in the face of Jesus Christ? Has it been the power of God unto *your* salvation? Thousands and tens of thousands upon earth own and rejoice in the excellency of its power. "Thanks be unto God," exclaims the Apostle, "which always causeth us to triumph in Christ, and maketh manifest the savour of his knowledge by us in every place. For we are unto God a sweet savour of Christ, in them that are saved, and in them that perish: to the one we are the savour of death unto death; and to the other the savour of life unto life. And who is sufficient for these things?"

Ah! who indeed is sufficient for such things? Earthen vessels have no sufficiency. We feel our weakness. We feel our nothingness. But our weakness, and our nothingness, have nothing to do with the lamp in the pitcher. We would press, then, your conscience for an answer. Are we a savour of life unto life, or a savour of death unto death unto you? What are the effects which our ministry is having upon you? We long for your salvation. We are not satisfied – how can we be? – with darkness and death. We shrink from the thought of appearing as witnesses in the court of heaven against one of those who hear our voice, or read our words. We labour – it is our earnest prayer, that you may be our hope, our joy, our crown of rejoicing in the presence of the Lord Jesus Christ at his coming. We can be satisfied with nothing short of this. Will anything short of this satisfy *you?* The saving conversion of your heart by the power of the Holy Ghost, the perfect and abiding pardon of your sins, your present acceptance of God in the righteousness of Jesus Christ, your deliverance from the power and love of sin – your growth in grace – your ripening for glory – these are the marks which prove the power of the Gospel in the earthen vessel. These are the happy effects for which the trumpets sound forth their notes, and for which the lamps shine in earthen pitchers. Let darkness reign – let the enemy muster all his hosts to battle, – *he* will be more than conqueror who obeys the trumpet's call, and walking in the light of the Lord, engages in the conflict for eternity with no other weapon in his hand, than "THE SWORD OF THE LORD, AND OF GIDEON."

8

The Victory Won

They "held the lamps in their left hands, and the trumpets in
their right hands to blow withal: and they cried, *The sword of
the Lord, and of Gideon* ... And the Lord set every man's sword
against his fellow, even throughout all the host: and all the host
ran, and cried, and fled. And there fell one hundred and twenty
thousand men that drew sword."
(Judges 7:20-22; 8:10)

"Soldier, rise – the war is done:
　Lo, the hosts of hell are flying,
'Twas thy Lord the battle won,
　Jesus vanquished them by dying.
Pass the stream – before thee lies
　All the conquered land of glory;
Hark! – what songs of rapture rise,
　These proclaim the victor's story.
　　Soldier, lay thy weapons down,
　　Quit the sword and take the crown:
Triumph! All thy foes are banished,
Death is slain, and hell has vanished."

ASSURANCE of victory steels the brave soldier's heart against
danger, nerves his right hand as he grasps his trusty sword, and
fires his valorous eye as he meets the enemy.

The true Christian is a true soldier. His heart needs strength,
his right hand nerve, his eye assurance of final victory. His Lord,
the Captain of his salvation, knows all this. Standing at the head
of his followers, He bids them all remember the high commission
which He, as their leader, hath received, "A bruised reed shall he

not break, and a smoking flax shall he not quench, till he send forth judgment UNTO VICTORY."

One of the soldiers of the army of faith – he was a standard-bearer of the cross – heard his Captain's voice, and raising high the banner of faith, in the face of assembled foes, shouted defiance – "O death, where is thy sting? O grave, where is thy victory?" And then, in full assurance of conquest, imagining death to be as silent as the grave, and the grave robbed of his spoils, he lifted up his voice again, in triumph, and sang – "Thanks be to God, *which giveth us the victory* through our Lord Jesus Christ." (*1 Corinthians 15:55-57*).

But our Captain does far more than animate his soldiers with assurance of final victory. As King of kings, and Lord of lords, He has already broken through the phalanxed hosts of the enemy – wrenched the sword from his hand – trampled his colours in the dust – "led captivity captive, and received gifts for men." He no longer wars himself in the dread battlefield. With his vesture dipped in blood, "He hath ascended up on high." From his lofty throne He beholdeth his faithful followers warring in the plain, and reaping the fruits of his victory. As Moses stood on the top of the hill, with the rod of God in his hand, and with outstretched arms encouraged Israel until they had conquered Amalek, so standeth our mighty Lord on the top of the mountain of glory, and with many a crown, and many a recompense in his right hand. He doth cheer and encourage his Israel, to go on conquering and to conquer. Behold that hand, and hear his loud voice, as its commands are caught up by his followers, and sent by them throughout all their ranks.

Despatch after despatch is published. Proclamation after proclamation – order after order is given. Every word is dictated by the Lord's own lips, and inscribed in the court of heaven, by the Holy Spirit himself. Each message bears the seal of his own signet, the sign of the cross. Every despatch is written with crimson ink drawn from veins opened on Calvary's hill.

And thus the despatches run, with but little intermission of time. So full is the overflowing heart of the Conqueror, that He longs for his people to "enter into the joy of their Lord."

The *first despatch*, embellished with a palm branch, runneth thus – "*To him that overcometh* will I give to eat of *the tree of life*, which is in the midst of the paradise of God."

The *second despatch*, to take away all fear of death – "*He that over-cometh*, shall not be *hurt of the second death.*"

The *third despatch*, to assure each warrior that his Captain's eye is upon him, and that He knoweth his name – "*To him that overcometh* will I give to *eat of the hidden manna*, and will give him *a white stone*, and in the stone a *new name written*, which no man knoweth saving he that receiveth it.*"

The *fourth despatch*, to show the wide extent of his dominions, and to assure each faithful warrior that he shall *live and reign* with Him – "*He that overcometh*, and keepeth my works unto the end, to him *will I give power over the nations.*"

The *fifth despatch*, to make known that each conqueror will find his place prepared at the Marriage Feast of the Lamb – "*He that over-cometh*, the same shall be clothed in *white raiment.*"

The *sixth despatch*, to proclaim the stability of his reign, and of the unchangeable happiness of every brave soldier – "*Him that over-cometh* will I make a *pillar* in the temple of my God.*"

The *seventh despatch*, to cheer and animate the whole band of warriors, with the example of the noblest endurance, and the richest recompense – "*To him that overcometh* will I grant to *sit with me in my throne*, even as I also overcame, and am set down with my Father in his throne.*"

The *eighth and final despatch*, to stimulate the souls of the belligerents, from their deepest depths – to awaken the highest ambition, of which mortal man is capable – to inspire the entire army with the prospect of the most imperishable glory and honour – "*He that over-cometh* shall inherit all things, and I WILL BE HIS GOD, AND HE SHALL BE MY SON." (See *Revelation 2:7, 11, 17, 26; 3:5, 12, 21; 21:7*).

What more can be needed? The forces of the enemy are indeed many, skilful, and mighty. Once they carried the war, even up to the palace of the Great King, and made havoc around the throne. Yea, they aimed at the usurpation of universal monarchy. Mighty principalities and powers were they, "rulers of darkness, and spiritual wickedness in high places." (*Ephesians 6:12*). But Omnipotence spake the word, and, as seared leaves in the forest, nipped by the Autumn frost, fall to rise no more, so "The angels which kept not their first estate, left their own habitation, and are reserved in everlasting chains under darkness unto the judgment of the great day." (*Jude 6*).

Their execution is delayed. They are "reserved in chains," to grace the final triumphs of their Conqueror. He permits them still to wage war against Him in a lower field. Thus they forge new chains of fire to bind themselves down hereafter. What depths of wisdom are here! Eternal ages, and worlds peopling immensity, will, "in that day," with one loud voice proclaim the justice of Jehovah!

Be it so, then, that our battle is not yet over. We look forward with joy unspeakable to the result. "They make war with the Lamb, and THE LAMB SHALL OVERCOME THEM: for He is Lord of lords, and King of kings: and they that are with Him are called, and chosen, and faithful." (*Revelation 17:14*).

The youngest soldier of the cross, the feeblest warrior in the army of the Lamb, the most trembling of his "chosen and faithful" followers, need dread no mighty foe. "Greater is He that is in you, than he that is in the world." (*1 John 4:4*). One brave leader felt this; and, grasping the standard of the cross, and waving it over his head, marked with the scars of many a battle, and treading in the footsteps of the Great Captain, he thus pressed forward to victory, and gave the watchword to the "chosen and faithful" – "Who shall separate us from the love of Christ? Shall tribulation, or distress, or persecution, or famine, or nakedness, or peril, or sword? As it is written, For thy sake we are killed all the day long; we are accounted as sheep for the slaughter. Nay, in all these things we are MORE THAN CONQUERORS, through Him that loved us." (*Romans 8:35-37*).

Let us now descend once more into the valley of Jezreel. We mark the *three hundred* – a brave band, following a brave leader.

We have seen some portion of their equipment, and observed their strange weapons of war – *trumpets* and *pitchers*.

In watching the closing scene we have three things to consider: 1. *Their lamps held forth.* 2. *The watchword of the night.* 3. *The victory won.*

The Lamps Held Forth

The pitchers contained the lamps. It was for the sake of the lamps, that the pitchers were brought into the battlefield. We have seen that the pitchers were made for the lamps, and not the lamps for the pitchers. The lamps, however, would have done little service but for the pitchers. When the pitchers had done their duty they were broken and cast aside. It was then that the lamps shone forth.

The sudden blazing forth of three hundred lamps in that dark night, amid the din of the crashing of pitchers, the sounding of trumpets, and raising the loud shout – "The sword of the Lord, and of Gideon" – was well calculated to awaken alarm and terror, and throw into hopeless confusion a surprised army, just awaking out of sleep. The Midianites were surrounded by these nocturnal visitors. These mysterious lamps magnified dangers. Their lights were enough to dazzle the eyes, and confuse the minds of the sleepers, but not enough to enable them to distinguish friend from foe. The sword once drawn in mistake, the whole army fell before it.

What an emblem are these lamps of the Word of the living God! In the dread conflict with the powers of darkness, the feeblest warrior may truly say, "Thy word is *a lamp* unto my feet, and a light unto my path." "I have ordained," saith the Lord, "a lamp for mine anointed." This lamp, though held in earthen vessels, shines brightest in the darkest night. It shows the believer the ambushes of the enemy. It points out to him where the serpent is lying coiled up, and ready to inflict a deadly wound. One great warrior thus entered his experience in the journal of his spiritual life – "By the words of thy lips I have kept me from the paths of the destroyer." (*Psalm 17:4*). And a greater Captain than he, and engaged in a more terrible conflict, held up this lamp in the face of the enemy, and defied him on the spot, and said, "It is written" – "It is written" – "It is written again;" and the enemy fled. That lamp carried confusion, dismay, terror, and ruin into the hosts of darkness. And when thus the Conqueror overcame, angels came and ministered unto Him; and doubtless, the echoes of their trumpets of victory thrilled through the hearts of their companions in glory. It is this lamp, so honoured, so potent in its effects, which the Captain of our salvation places in the hand of each of his followers! How great the charge, how rich the loan! Were each one of us to "hold forth the Word of life" – *to hold it up*, faithfully and courageously, as the one only lamp to guide the sinner out of darkness into light – as the one only lamp which can give a fixed and certain light, amid all the watch-fires of the enemy, we should do far more execution against the powers of darkness than is now being done. Were soldiers of the cross wiser, we should be more bold in breaking to pieces the earthen pitchers of man's moulding, and be more earnest in lifting high, above the heads of all men, the *naked lamp* of the Word of God. We want to see this lamp – clear in its own light, distinct in its own brightness – in the hand of every warrior, be he standing at his post, in private, or in public; in the school, or in the pulpit, in business, or in the senate, on the platform, or at the press. Let this lamp engirdle the world, now sleeping in darkness, and lying in the wicked one, and the final victory of grace will soon be proclaimed!

But it is a solemn and transparent truth that *the same lamp which leads one man to victory, often leads another to death.* The thousands of the Midianites fell in the light of those lamps, which saved the three hundred followers of Gideon. If men be found fighting on the wrong side, and in spite of the light which shineth upon them, continue to do so, the lamp will confound, confuse, and cause them to fall by their own swords on the field of battle. One of the most fearful of deaths is that of suicide, when a man becomes his own executioner, and quenches, with his own hand, the spark of life which God hath given him, and rushes unbidden into the presence of his Maker. And just such an one is he, who, receiving the lamp of the Word, quenches its light in his own bosom. He is said to "wrest the Scriptures unto his own destruction." (*2 Peter 3:16*). Better far, for such an one had he never been born!

The Watchword of the Night

Now listen to the watchword of the night – "*The sword of the Lord, and of Gideon.*" *Where*, we might ask, was this sword? Surely not in the hand of Gideon, nor in the hands of his brave three hundred! They held in their hands nothing but pitchers, and lamps, and trumpets! What, then, was the meaning of the shout, intended to inspire each true heart with new courage – "The sword of the Lord, and of Gideon"?

Israel knew not, nor did Israel's leader, *what* sword the Lord would draw from its scabbard that night. They could not tell, in what wonderful way, the Lord would subdue their enemies under them. There was but one mighty and trusty sword on which Gideon *could* safely rely, and on which, as we have already seen, he *did* rely – the Word of God – the promises of a faithful God. It was *that* sword which his hand of faith grasped! It was in the power of *that* sword only, he taught his followers to trust. We saw him on the high rock, where now stands his altar; and again in the barn floor, where lies his fleece of wool; and on both occasions proving the trusty nature of this wondrous sword. He would not move an inch until he had proved it. Over and over again, did he examine it; and, at length, being satisfied that there was not a single flaw in it, that it was welded and tempered in the armoury of heaven, he placed it in the hands of his valorous three hundred; and, whilst to the eye of some, nothing could be seen in their hands, but trumpets and pitchers, a two-edged sword was theirs, before whose keen edge even Satan had fallen; and as they brake their pitchers and held forth their lamps, he taught them to proclaim aloud their faith – "The sword of the Lord, and of Gideon!"

If we would be conquerors, we too must grasp, with the hand of faith, the same invincible and invisible sword. We must go into battle and make mention of no other. How potent is it! Did ever a mortal rely on it, and fail? Did ever an angel trust in it in vain? Surely it was when Satan and his mad followers lost hold of this sword in heaven, that they lost allegiance to God, and all power to war against Him. It was, too, when Adam's firm grasp relaxed, and this sword dropped upon the green sward in Eden, that the enemy came in like a flood, and there was no power left to withstand him. And will not the final victory over the subtle "accuser of the brethren" be won by the same mighty sword? Do we not read that the redeemed "overcame him by the blood of the Lamb, and *by the word of their testimony*"?

Here, then, is the source of the believer's strength. The veriest babe is mighty, if his feeble hand do but lie upon the hilt of this sword. None dare touch him; none dare disturb. That sword, like the fiery sword at Eden's gates, turneth every way. It keepeth and guardeth the tree of life, and everyone who is gathering of its healing leaves and luscious fruits. Soldier of the cross! do battle with this sword in your hand, and you will do exploits. You need no other weapon of warfare. Keep it bright; let it not rust in its scabbard. Often, often prove its metal. Learn well the sword-exercise by practical experience. The lessons drawn from the schools will profit you but little, in real conflict. You must learn real war in the experience of the field. Behold, the trumpet sounds! War is declared. The enemy is at his post. Many have fallen, and are falling still, before his fiery darts. Heaps upon heaps of slain, cause the earth to groan under their burden. Death – the death of sin – stalks the wide world over. The Goliath of mighty hosts bids defiance to the armies of the living God! Up, soldier! either he, or you, must fall in the deadly strife. *There* is your enemy; mark him well! He cometh on apace! He strides towards you, he looks around, he disdainfully despises you. He curses you by all the gods in hell! Now, arise; run to meet him; draw the sword of the Spirit! Wield it in faith, and he will fall before the shout of the armies of the cross – "The sword of the Lord, and of Gideon."

The Victory Won

Dreams are usually foolish things, the effects of an excited state of the mind, or of a disordered condition of the body.

But the Lord often chooses the most unlikely means for the accomplishment of his own wise and gracious purposes. He has not infrequently conveyed his will through the medium of dreams. When Joseph was in Egypt's prison, his liberation was brought about by his interpretation of Pharaoh's dreams. The interpretation of a dream, was appointed by the Lord as a means of strength to Gideon's faith. At the word of the Lord, Gideon took his servant Phurah, and went down to the sleeping host of the Midianites. There he heard a man tell his dream to his fellow: "Behold, I dreamed a dream, and lo, a cake of barley bread tumbled into the host of Midian, and came unto a tent, and smote it that it fell, and overturned it, that the tent lay along." This was the dream, and apparently a more unmeaning one can scarcely be imagined. But the Lord put the true interpretation of it into the mouth of the dreamer's companion, who said, "This is nothing else save the sword of Gideon, the son of Joash, a man of Israel; for into his hand God hath delivered Midian, and all the host." (*Judges 7:9-14*). This was enough for Gideon. He believed this additional sign which God gave him, to assure him of victory. He at once ordered the battle, as we have already seen. And when "the three companies blew the trumpets, and brake the pitchers, and held the lamps in their left hands, and the trumpets in their right hands, to blow withal, and cried, The sword of the Lord and of Gideon," the "barley cake" *did* "tumble into the hosts of Midian," and overthrew them, for it came to pass, that "the host ran, and cried, and fled. And the three hundred blew the trumpets, and the Lord set every man's sword against his fellow, even throughout all the host" … And "there fell an hundred and twenty thousand men that drew sword." (*Judges 7:20-22; 8:10*).

Two Great Lessons

We learn from the whole subject:

1. A voice is heard over this field of victory, and its sweet cadences are echoed from every hill of promise, saying, "*Not by might, nor by power, but by my Spirit, saith the Lord.*"

The youngest child in Israel could run and read the meaning of Gideon's victory. Man was nothing that day, and God was everything. The victory was wholly his. His sword alone smote down the enemy. This He made apparent. Thus it is that the Lord will make his hand to appear, in the salvation of the soul. He will bring down the pride of man. He will lay it in the dust. He will convince the sinner of his own utter weakness, and bring him to despair of all help in himself, and then He will place his two-edged sword of promise in his hand, and make him more than conqueror.

2. We learn, also, that *no one who puts his trust in the Lord shall be confounded.* Gideon's victory was a victory of faith. He had nothing to rest upon, but the Word of the Lord. He trusted *that*, he was valiant in *that*, and was victorious. God honours faith. It is that grace, which, above all others, honours God. "Without faith it is impossible to please God." He loves confidence in his promises. He places this sword in the soldier's hand to be relied upon; to be made his own, so that he might say, "The sword of the Lord, and MINE. I have no other sword; I know of no other. This, and this only, is the LORD'S. And this, and this only, is MINE." It is this faith which makes one man differ from another, and the rejoicing believer from himself, in fear and doubt. It was faith which made Peter walking on the water, and saying, "Lord, bid me come to thee," differ from Peter sinking, and crying, "Lord, save me, I perish." It is this faith which strengthens the weakest and youngest babe in Christ to wax valiant in fight, and overcome that world before whom giants have fallen. For "who is he that overcometh the world, but he that believeth that Jesus is the Son of God?"

Such a believer conquers. He *conquers sin*, by bathing his leprous soul in the full fountain, drawn from the stream which flowed from the Smitten Rock on Calvary. He *overcomes the law* – the condemning power of a broken, violated, and pursuing, and unbending law – by wrapping around his soul the soldier's cloak of righteousness, even the righteousness of Immanuel, which is unto all and upon all them that believe, without any difference; and thus he turns round and faces the law, and defies it to condemn him, or to find fault with him. He *overcomes death*, the last enemy; for, taking the rod of Christ upon his shoulder, his cross for a staff in his left hand, and the sword of the Spirit in his right hand, he can march forward calmly, down into the valley, and, as he walks, he can unfurl his banner, on which is inscribed "*Jehovah-shalom;*" and, waving this banner over his head, he can catch up the war-cry of one who has gone before: "Yea, though I walk through the valley of the shadow of death, I will fear no evil: for THOU ART WITH ME; thy rod and thy staff they comfort me."

We want this victory. We are all waging a war, the issues of which will be eternal. Soon, soon the trumpets will sound. Soon the grand muster-roll will be called over. Soon every soul will have to stand up in his place, and answer to his name. There will be no going back to one's home, or to one's fireside then. There will be no discharge from that day of decision. The three hundred will be there. There, too, will be the 9,700, and the 22,000 also! No one will appear as proxy for his fellow. Every man will answer for himself. Alone we shall all stand. And when thus we stand, all the past of our lives will come rushing up before our vision. Memory will awaken from her slumbers, and scenes long forgotten will arise before us. Secret and public acts, words and deeds, thoughts and feelings, will then all appear as fresh as on the day which gave them birth. A thousand years will be as one day. Enemies, too, the arch-accusers of the brethren, will be there. The subtle tempters to sin, and the faithful preachers of righteousness, will stand on either side. Angels, holy and bright, archangels and cherubims, thrones and dominions will be there, to watch, to divide, to separate, before the clock of eternity shall strike. Blackness and darkness will gather over the left-hand side of the throne. "The wrath of the Lamb" will begin to crimson that countenance, once bedewed with tears of melting tenderness. His eyes will be as flames of fire; judgment will issue from his holy lips: "He that is unjust, let him be unjust still: and he that is filthy, let him be filthy still." And then, oh! what "railing accusations" will swell from every enraged heart. "Every man's sword will be set against his fellow, even throughout all the host," and the host will flee! They will flee! And, oh! that flight which will then take place! "O my soul, come not thou into their secret: unto their assembly, mine honour, be not thou united." Away, away will they flee, "from the presence of the Lord, and from the glory of his power." Deeper, deeper still, into the dark depths of eternal perdition!

We cannot follow them! No! We would not if we could!

But silver trumpets will still sound around the throne. The lamps of heaven, of life, of bliss, of glory, will drive all darkness from before them. All brightness will shine on the right side of the throne. The bow of the covenant will be seen "round about it." Harpers will be there, with golden harps. The voice of many waters will be heard, amid the shout of triumph. Sweet music will swell through the courts of heaven. "A new song" will be sung, by ten thousand times ten thousand. It will be repeated, caught up, and sung again, and again. Oh! that chorus of praise which will burst forth from every side! Not a tongue will be mute! Palms of victory will wave from every hand. The armour of the soldier will now be laid aside. The wardrobe of heaven will now be wide opened. Each conqueror will be arrayed in "white robes." Will any voice enquire, "*Who* are they? Whence came they?" The beloved disciple, leaning on the Saviour's bosom, will answer, "Sir, thou knowest." And then will one reply, and say, "These are they who came out of great tribulation, and have washed their robes, and made them white in the blood of the Lamb." We cannot mistake them. They are the soldiers of the cross. They have fought the good fight. They have laid hold on eternal life. "They loved not their lives unto the death."

The battle is over. The victory is won. They enter into the joy of their Lord. Angels and cherubim are now their companions and friends. Yea, He that sitteth on the throne, now dwelleth among them. Their cup is full. It runneth over. An "eternal weight of glory" is theirs. Faith has triumphed. The Church is saved. The Triune Jehovah is glorified.

And could we but catch the key-note of that "new song" of victory, which will then ascend before the throne, ascribing all praise unto the Captain of our Salvation, saying, "Worthy is the Lamb that was slain to receive power, and riches, and wisdom, and strength, and honour, and glory, and blessing," we should even now, in the field of battle, take down our harps from the willows, and raise our voices, in harmony with the music of heaven.

Our song is one, whether we mingle with the shining ones above, or do battle with war-clad warriors below. THE VALOUR OF FAITH is a felt reality now. Hereafter, it will be a matter of joyous remembrance. *Faith* would gladly lay aside her arms, and lie down for ever, in peace, at the foot of the throne. She would fain give place to love, which abideth for ever. But no grace could ever stand in the battlefield without her broad shield and mighty sword. Here she is all potent, and none can withstand the shock of her onslaught. This we have seen in the history before us. May the reader and the writer experience its truth together, and together stand on the hill of glory, with the standard of the cross waving over our heads, with this inscription upon it, engraven in characters of light:

"THIS IS THE VICTORY THAT OVERCOMETH THE WORLD, EVEN OUR FAITH."